I0418004

You Can't Hurt Me Anymore:

A Memoir

Written by:

C.A. Russell

Table of Contents

Preface

This book is a memoir and autobiographical in nature. Names and details have been changed to protect identities. Events recorded are based on my point of view, and my present recollections of experiences over time. Others may have a different perception of these events. I'm not reliving history here — I'm making herstory. This is a story of hope; a story of overcoming trauma and rising from domestic violence. This is <u>my</u> story.

ACKNOWLEDGEMENTS

I would like to thank everyone who worked tirelessly with me on this book. My editor, Hannah Luera, who helped make this a reality, made me dig deeper than I ever thought I could to bring this to life, and stood by me every step of the way. Thank you doesn't seem like enough. My publishing consultant, Chynna Creative Co. who made it possible to get this into the hands of anyone who needs this or could benefit from this. To both of you, thank you for believing in me. The whole team at Designed.co who brought my vision for a cover to life. To Becky Colvin, Boudica Marketing for helping with the promotion and marketing of this book, and to my legal team, thank you for your contributions.

I would like to thank my children. Without them, I would not have had the strength to fight this battle and win this war. They are the true heroes of my life, and to all three of you, I am eternally grateful I get to be your mom. To my husband. Who loved me even in my worst, and who picked up the pieces of my brokenness and waited as patiently as he could for me to heal, who showed me what true love, what real love is supposed to look like. To anyone who has hurt me, thank you. For without those experiences, I never would have known my true strength. I never would have realized that I am enough exactly as I am. To all of my readers and supporters, I am humbly thankful for all of you.

AUTHOR NOTES

This book was hard to write. The problem was not finding the words but finding the emotional vulnerability to open myself up like this for the world to see. I've never been an open book. I'm just a girl with a broken smile who puts on a brave face and handles it. I am perfectly me. I'm not without my flaws, and I definitely have imperfections, but at the end of the day, I am proud of who I have become. And I fought hard to be okay with who I am, to fully understand that nobody is perfect, but I love myself as I am. It took a long time to come to that realization. Decades. The constant yammering in my ear that I am not good enough, I will never amount to anything or that I am utterly useless left me feeling defeated for more than half my life. It wasn't until I was at my lowest point with no fight left in me that I decided I get to choose.

I chose my path. Sometimes I wonder what my life would look like now if I had made a different decision 30 years ago, or 20 years ago, or even 10 years ago. I'll get into each of these decisions throughout this book, but each choice leads down a different road. Sometimes I think about it and wonder if I had any say at all. Sometimes I took a wrong turn, but I knew when to detour. I made U-turns, turned left when I should have turned right, illegally backed up, and hit a few parked cars along the way, but I ended up exactly where I needed to be. It just took me a bit longer to get there.

I've suffered through (and survived) emotional trauma, different kinds of abuse, neglect and abandonment, depression, anxiety, and complete despair. Hitting every jagged edge on the way to rock bottom; both of my own doing and at the hands of someone else; I became completely despondent and gained a dependence on finding acceptance and praise everywhere I went. This landed me in a position I never thought I would find myself in. I clawed my way back to the surface. I will be the first to say that is a feat of pure determination and grit I never knew I had. I was a weak, shy, clumsy, and introverted adolescent who grew into a fierce, strong, motivated, and mentally powerful woman who can do anything. As I stare into the mirror, willing myself to write this, I realize sometimes your reflection will tell you exactly who you are. What do I see staring back at me? What do I want to see? With all the destruction burning around me, I geared myself up to rise from the ashes. Without this experience, I would never be able to write this in the hopes of reaching one person who needs to hear it. I am enough. I am worthy. I am loved. And so are you.

CHAPTER ONE

The Day I Started Living - *Age 29*

It was early 2011. I had just settled into my shady two-bedroom apartment. It was the first time in my life that I had lived alone. I had three young children sleeping in the next room, but I was alone. I felt free and unshackled yet cramped and tense at the same time. I hadn't had a decent night's sleep in months. We had no furniture. A small TV, a futon mattress, and an empty pizza box cluttered the corner of the room. I couldn't tell if it was the living room or the dining room. The bags under my eyes could hold groceries. I splashed water on my face and tried to look refreshed, then frowned. The fact that I was a 29-year-old single mom trying to get her life together could be the culprit, I suppose. Or it could be the hard-headed, alcoholic, abusive, self-loathing, self-righteous, tyrant bully I called my children's father.

I picked my phone up off the floor, exactly where I'd left it after receiving a plethora of messages telling me what an awful person I am. *"Nobody else will want you. Nobody will do for you what I did for you. You're a used-up single mom, a terrible one at that. You're a waste of space."* The last message had sent me into a downward spiral; I had thrown my phone, guzzled a glass of wine, and cried myself to sleep. That turned out to be a typical Sunday night for him. Sunday became the night he had a few and sent drunk texts to his ex-wife. They were a brutal mind-warp. If only I knew then that they'd get much worse. A cup of coffee, a little eyeliner, some lip gloss, and a shrug of my shoulders meant it was the best the day was going to get.

Getting my daughter out of bed was much like folding up a tent and trying to put it back into its carrying bag. It starts out well, but you end up getting frustrated, cramming it in, and settling for it halfway hanging out of the bag. At least it's where it's supposed to go.

"Please, Chloe, you must get out of bed! We're going to be late!"

Both boys started to rustle and the baby started crying. I tended to him, changed his diaper, threw a onesie on him, and popped the pacifier in his mouth. I smiled at him, knowing at 18 months old, he won't remember these hard times. Noah, my three-year-old, toddles over to me, throws himself around my leg, and proceeds to scream at the top of his lungs for no apparent reason. My 8-year-old daughter has fallen asleep on top of the box that has all her clothes in it. It's supposed to be her first day at a new school.

I shouted at her. *"It's time to wake up!"*

I didn't have the highest patience level in the world. I reminded myself I should work on that. First, though, I needed to get this child in school and the boys in daycare. It was my first day at a temp job, and I wanted to make a good impression. I hadn't had a job since college, and I was nervous. I was starting over for the second time in my life, and this time, I struggled to believe I would overcome this. The last two weeks were a blur. Still in fight-or-flight mode, constantly looking over my shoulder, and sensing danger around every corner, I didn't know how to relax. I still slept with my shoes on. My dad had died a few weeks prior and I hadn't even had time to grieve. The remaining dollars in his bank account had gotten me into this apartment. I was making calls to every complex in the area during the entire four-hour drive, and this was the only place that had an available unit within the week. Completely humbled and grateful for life-long family friends who allowed us to crash in their guest room until my apartment was ready, I knew I had to figure out my next steps on my own. Grabbing the keys to the Buick — the only physical asset I had left from my father —- we scurried out the door. Heading back to my hometown with my tail between my legs was defeating. Even if nobody else blamed me, I certainly did. Is this how the "good girl" had turned out? The one with a promising future and her head on straight?

As we dawdled out of the house, with Noah still attached to my leg, I pushed Chloe out the door with one foot as Liam sat on the opposite hip. With one shoe on, her backpack hanging off her shoulder, and her ponytail falling out, Chloe looked up at me. Her goofy grin with the top two teeth missing got me every time. I smiled for the first time in months. I was overwhelmed, but I breathed. These three little people depended on me. I was rushing and panicking, and they just breathed. Just a day in my life. A day I will never forget: the day I started living.

CHAPTER TWO

The Wrong Path with the Right Intentions - *Age 18*

I was a good teenager. I never snuck out, never went anywhere I wasn't supposed to, always came home at curfew, dated the same guy throughout high school, and held two jobs. I helped support my twin brothers who were eight years younger than me. I felt more like a second mom than their sister. They looked up to me. I occasionally talked back, went snooping around for things I shouldn't have, and stayed up way too late; but when I got in trouble, I learned my lesson. I hated getting yelled at or grounded. I felt small. And the guilt (whether I got caught or not) was punishment enough. I hated that feeling. It was not that I had the greatest upbringing or the strictest parents. The fear of abandonment or being shunned was far too great. I suffered such sorrow when I messed up, as all teenagers do at some point, but I felt gravely guilty when I misbehaved, so I rarely did it. In fact, I'm surprised I didn't end up on a totally different path. But that's where my strength shines.

I didn't have the proper tools, growing up. I knew the difference between right and wrong, but my role models were too self-absorbed to teach me. During these years, my father was lenient. He did the best he could with what he had. He was a recovering alcoholic. By the time I was a sophomore in high school, and it was just my brothers, my father and I, he was nine years sober. I was very proud of him, even if he wasn't always there for me. I barely knew him when I moved in with him, but we figured it out together. Although he didn't know the first thing about raising a teenage girl, he knew enough to keep me out of harm's way. He learned pretty quickly. We took turns, almost like roommates; doing dishes, the laundry, vacuuming. I got Friday nights out, he got Saturdays. It worked. My dad tried. He wasn't perfect, but he was mine. He did his best and it was enough for me. He fed me, gave me money, bought me clothes and books, and he listened. I trusted him, but at the time I didn't realize how sheltered I had been.

When I turned eighteen, graduated high school, and left for college, the goody-goody girl I'd always been disappeared. She just vanished. Driving down my street with my entire bedroom packed tightly into the Hyundai Elantra my dad bought me for graduation, I bawled my eyes out, but not because I was leaving home. It was partly because I was leaving safety, and my brothers whom I wished I could bring with me, but mostly it was because I was free. Free. Like a caged bird whose owner left the door open. I was loved and cared for and safe, but I had the entire world at my beck and call now.

Since I started college the summer immediately after graduation, there was no time to practice being an adult. I jumped right in. I was studious and strived to excel in everything but had zero life experience and quickly discovered that I had absolutely no idea what I was doing. After arriving at the college campus and meeting with my advisor, I realized I wasn't assigned a dorm room. Something about the deposit not being paid. I had earned the "Bright Futures" scholarship; one student from all of the area high schools representing the entire county won a full scholarship to any state university. "Everything will be taken care of." I assumed this meant housing and food. It did; I just had to allocate funds to it. As I said, my father was not equipped for a teenage girl, so he wasn't there to ease me into adulthood. My advisor helped me sublet an off-campus apartment from an upcoming senior who was interning for the summer. You would think with my 3.86 GPA, I would know what subletting meant. I wanted to go to law school but was focusing on English as my major first.

I remember my first college party. I was shy, a wallflower, and fully aware I didn't belong there. These partygoers were so much older than me, more mature and far cooler than I would ever be. Cell phones weren't quite so popular yet. They were more of a necessity. Instead of texting, I was literally twiddling my thumbs. I didn't like alcohol. I didn't like the way it behaved. Lowering inhibitions, or as Tommy said as he opened the bottle with his teeth and practically threw it at me, *"liquid courage."* Though I declined, he shouted *"at least hold it"* over the music. At least I felt like I looked cooler. I sat with him for a while. Tommy was a discernible frat boy: always a drink in hand, blatantly immature, but funny.

Two beers and I was drunk, and these attractive college boys were talking to me and making me laugh. Maybe this was a thing. Soon, I was skinny dipping in swimming pools, eating pizza at 4 AM, and dancing on tabletops. After that, the rest of my first year is a blur. I took on a full load of classes and maintained my GPA, but I partied hard and was rarely home. Without a need for a place of my own, and after getting locked out for non-payment, I put what little I owned in storage and slept wherever I ended up for the night, along with about 20 other college co-eds. There wasn't a single person to answer to. I was the adult. I was the one in charge, making all my own decisions.

I can recall my last college party, too, although I don't remember being there.

I was studying for a mid-term in the 24-hour on-campus library, sipping on a cappuccino, when my friend Rachel staggered in. *"It's my birthday. Jake's taking me to Roxy."* She sat in front of me in class. Her dark hair was always piled neatly in a bun, and she usually wore her campus sweatshirt and acid-washed blue jeans. Sophisticated and classy, she had it together during the week, or at least appeared to. She was a person I envied. We had walked into our first day of class at the same time and gone for the same seat: the back right corner, so nobody was staring at the back of my head. I hated feeling like anyone was staring at me. She laughed and told me to take it as she sat down directly in front of me. Our first assignment was to write a paper with another person on echoing subjects. We chose each other, so we spent many hours together. I stayed in her bedroom much of the time and she never really questioned it.

I slammed my book closed as she grabbed me by the arm. *"Help me get ready! You should come! You can wear my mini skirt,"* she said as she winked at me.

This particular night, Rachel looked stunning. Her long, chestnut, naturally wavy hair flowed effortlessly down the back of her little black dress, which revealed a toned back. She waltzed out of her room and smirked. *"You only turn 19 once."* Her boyfriend picked us up in his giant, obnoxiously loud, lifted pick-up truck. My 5'3" small-framed body couldn't even hoist myself up onto the built-in step stool to climb into the truck, and I wasn't about to try it in Rachel's miniskirt. She laughed at me the way she always laughed when I couldn't stand on my own two feet. She threw her head back, put her arm across her belly, and gave me a guttural laugh. Her laugh was contagious and it always made me giggle. She was 5'8" without the two inches from her heels, and she was all legs. She had no trouble hopping up into the massive vehicle. My towering friend clamped her hands together and let me step into them for the boost up into the truck. I distinctly remember the sound that truck made as it left me at the bar later that night.

Rachel met Jake at the college football game. He was a junior and had turned 21 over the summer. They were always together and I didn't want to be the third wheel, so I rarely joined them. Rachel was pretty, but she didn't know it. She didn't flaunt it anyway. He thought she was out of his league, but she liked him because he was a genuinely nice guy. He was taking her to the Roxy, an elite club downtown to celebrate her birthday. For whatever reason, this time, when Rachel asked me to join them, I was eager to tag along. Jake bought us drinks all night long. Rachel never left his side, and I never left hers. We danced, drank, laughed, and partied. I started to get a headache and wanted Rachel to go outside with me for some fresh air. *"We'll never get back in."* Rachel handed me a pill that I popped without questioning it. *"Here. Your headache will be gone in a few."* I naively trusted her.

The next thing I remember, I woke up in an apartment full of people. I didn't know a single one of them. I realized my skirt was missing, as were the heels I borrowed from Rachel. I was wearing a damp white t-shirt and my underwear. I searched every room for her and couldn't find her. I assumed she'd taken back the things I borrowed from her and went home, but I couldn't figure out why she would do that. My vision was fuzzy, and I couldn't imagine why she would have left me there, half-dressed. I couldn't find my phone or my wallet. I remembered having a clutch I wore on a chain like a necklace. Frantically grabbing at my neck, I found nothing there. I had no idea where I was, how I got there, or how I was going to get home. Wherever home was. I didn't even have a place to go "home" to.

I quickly learned we were three miles from campus, so I borrowed some sweatpants and hitched a ride. I walked to Rachel's apartment, but she wasn't home. Neither were either of her roommates. It was Saturday morning. Where did everybody end up? Jake's truck wasn't in her parking spot, so I guessed they were at his place. I had no idea where he lived.

I felt abandoned, betrayed, and completely alone. The guys that lived upstairs from Rachel were emptying out their trash from an apparent party at their place the night before. I asked if they'd seen her, and they invited me in for a drink. My head was pounding. *"It'll make you feel better."* I accepted. I stayed for six hours in that apartment, just talking, drinking, and forgetting. I ended up dating Rob, one of the guys that lived in that apartment, for four months until my entire world was turned upside down.

I had no access to my things. They were sporadically strewn around Rachel's apartment and other places I had crashed recently. I called Rachel from Rob's phone, but she didn't pick up. I crashed on his couch that night. The next morning, I asked him to take me to my storage unit so I could get some clothes and things for class, but then remembered my key was in the clutch I had misplaced. He bought me a campus t-shirt and gym shorts from the school store. He told me he'd see me later. I beamed, grateful. Rachel wasn't in class, which was discouraging. I went back to her apartment after class and she still wasn't home, so I knocked on Rob's door. He let me take a shower, and he fed me. Who was this guy next door? I thought all college guys were jerks. He gave me his bed that night, and he slept on the couch. That was the arrangement all week.

When I finally found Rachel three days later, she was severely hung over. I eventually discovered she had given me Xanax and I was horrified. She said that Jake had given it to her many times, and she thought it would help me have a fun time. Visibly upset, I asked her what happened.

I listened intently as she recalled what she knew. I took the pill and I sat back down at the bar. I still had a headache 45 minutes later, and I was rubbing my temple. She shoved a drink in my hand and introduced me to Jake's friend, Mark. Mark was gorgeous! He was a tall, dark-haired, blue-eyed, muscular, toned, tanned, beautiful piece of eye candy. He offered to take me outside to get some fresh air away from the loud, thumping music and I obliged, following him like a puppy dog. I stumbled across the dance floor to the exit, where he bent down and took off my high heels. Rachel said she came looking for me after some time, and it seemed like I felt better. Mark invited us to an after-party, and we wanted to go. *"It's still my birthday, let's go!"*. She had to get Jake, so she'd told us, *"Stay here! I'll help you up in a minute."* She was referring to the truck. It was then I handed her my phone and necklace clutch. They came out arguing because Jake didn't want to go to a party. Rachel usually got what she wanted, so I didn't worry. I could hear them yelling at each other and then the diesel roar as they drove away, probably still arguing.

"You left me-" I started to say.

"You had his motorcycle helmet in your hand." That didn't sound like me at all. *"Your headache was gone,"* she shrugged.

"You were supposed to bring me back. I went to your place looking for you." I was angry.

"You didn't seem too afraid to go with him, but I hadn't realized I had your phone," She apologetically stammered.

I was appalled and upset with myself. This wasn't something I had ever done before. I tried to put the pieces of the night together and I could barely remember the house full of people. So full, I could barely move around. Everything was blurry like I was looking through a window underwater. I remembered a guy screaming in my face, but what he was saying and why, I couldn't recall. Rachel and Jake met up with some other friends and they took "many more pills," she confided. The image of my perfect, straight-and-narrow, ideal friend was severely tarnished. After returning my cell phone and clutch, she hugged me. *"I'm sorry. Meet me at my place. We have that paper due next week."* She half-smiled and sulked off to get breakfast and coffee.

I went back to Rob's, and we had our first real date outside the apartment. I couldn't shake the feeling of uneasiness. I felt betrayed by Rachel. It wasn't entirely her fault, but everything I thought I knew, and everything I trusted, was wrong. Rob and I ended up in the park near the huge lake at the recreation center, and we talked for hours. He let me vent and cry and complain. We watched the sun come up. Walking back to his apartment, he kissed me. We slept in the same bed for the first time. I stayed there when he was in class, and he left his door unlocked so I could come back after class. I teetered back and forth between his apartment and Rachel's for several weeks.

I was starting to have real feelings for Rob when the rug got pulled out from under me. I was late!

I went to the campus clinic and they gave me a pregnancy test. Positive! They gave me a blood test for further diagnosis. About 6 weeks!! I started exclusively seeing Rob about that long ago. Trying to do the math, it wasn't adding up. I hadn't been with anyone else in nearly a year. They had to be wrong. Could it have happened like that? I ignored Rob's calls for the next two days and hid in Rachel's room. I skipped class and tried to wrap my head around this. I had no idea what I was going to do, or what I was doing with my life. I needed to figure something out before I told anyone. I certainly wasn't going to tell my dad. Rachel came out of the bathroom in her towel with her earphones in. She was holding a brush like a microphone and singing, *"You Got to Fight for Your Right to Party"* by the Beastie Boys. A flashback hit me like a freight train from that weird night I couldn't remember.

"You got to fight, for your right, to paaaaarrrrty" I was standing in the kitchen talking to some random guy about who knows what. I remembered Mark whispering in my ear. Bits and pieces came back to me, but I still couldn't fill in the blanks. I vaguely remembered dancing on a tabletop with a ton of other people.

I finally called Rob. He was extremely supportive and understanding, considering the circumstances. I kept having flashbacks of that night over the next few weeks. One night in early November, I woke up screaming. Cold sweats, my heart pounding.

Dancing on top of the table, thrusting my hips, flailing my arms around to Bon Jovi. How is this table holding so many people? People are groping and making out with each other. Someone grabbed my arm and helped me off the table. "Wet t-shirt contest" shouted in my ear. "I don't have a t-shirt!" I exclaimed. Mark peeled off my red peplum shirt with black lace going down the back and exchanged it for the white t-shirt he wore under his button-up. The black pleather mini skirt I was wearing was completely covered by the shirt. A row of girls in white t-shirts were standing in the kitchen as the guys came up one by one to throw water and beer on us. The Beastie Boys were blaring through the speakers. "DANCE!!!" we were instructed after another toss of liquid turned the t-shirts into a peep show. I hazily remembered someone asking me if I wanted to share a shower. And then a guy on top of me. Then another. Then someone screaming at me to shut up with his face inches from mine.

Pain? A forearm pressed against my face, pinning my head to the floor. Shivering. Trembling. Fear or cold: the feeling was uncertain. Fine line between predator and prey. Innocence lost. Safety compromised. Overpowering. Overbearing. Overcome. Thirst for lust. Hunger for desire. Yearning for affection. At someone's cost. At my cost. My naïveté, gullibility, and corruptibility were evident. The cold, hard floor against my back. The force of a forearm strewn across my face. My lip pressed against my tooth, unable to move my head; the pinching. The metallic taste of blood. Fading in and out of awareness. My voice constricted; stifled. Trying to cry out, push up, or just move my head a quarter of an inch: restricted. One guy. Another guy. A third guy.

Another. Another? The lowly grunt in my ear that caused me to cringe. Then, the distinctly different tone of a male voice moaning above my head. The feeling of a hand on my ankle. One on my thigh. Another on my arm, and yet another on my head, not including the forearm still pinning my head to the ground. My ear folded on top of itself, crushed into the cold tile. One person could not touch me in all these places at once, so I was aware there was more than one. A single tear pooled at the corner of my eye and inched its way towards my ear. A muffled moan caught in the back of my throat escaped my crushed lips. "SHUT UP!" one of them whispered with a grunt as he turned his head slightly towards mine so he could wipe his forehead with the arm that was still compressing my face. Spittle spewed as he hissed at me. Pain seared through my body. Tension built. The walls closed in. The room spun. 'Stop!' I screamed in my head. 'No,' the agony as I tried to turn my face to escape the grasp. The encapsulating anguish. Ten minutes felt like 90. The glow of a black light on the stark white ceiling; I tried to count the popcorn pieces to drown it out. Pressure. The feeling of complete helplessness. Darkness. Squeezing my eyes shut, I escaped to a safe place, only to be brought back by a zipper digging into my upper thigh. Burning. Scorching. I inhaled a woodsy scent. The heady smell of pine and patchouli infiltrated my nostrils. The musky masculinity assaulted my senses and I passed out as a submissive murmur escaped me.

I'm in pure panic. I was gang-raped at that party. I most likely got pregnant during that escapade. I was to blame. I was the only one at fault. Rob just hugged me as I sobbed and tried to recollect the events of that night. He took me to campus security. I told them what supposedly happened. Since it'd been several weeks, there was no evidence. I didn't even know where this happened or who was there. I remembered Mark's name, but I hardly remembered his face. I probably wouldn't have recognized him if I passed by him. I couldn't even be sure he was involved, other than knowing he was in the house and that's how I got there. All they did was perform a blood panel to check for STDs, which was negative, thank goodness. Completely mortified and disgusted with myself, I seriously considered my next steps. Rob stayed by my side during this whole ordeal as it came to light in my head. I still didn't remember all the details, but some parts became very real. Within days, I made the heart-wrenching decision to get an abortion. It wasn't an easy decision, and I still think about the moment when I decided to do it. Rob was amazing throughout.

"What if it's mine?" he asked me on our way to the clinic.

"What if it isn't?" I pleaded. Plus, nothing says forever for a new relationship like a baby. He paid for the procedure and held my hand the entire time.

Bright white light. A spotlight of regret and shame on me; I wasn't a party girl. This was my scarlet letter, or at least it felt that way. Completely alone except for the squeeze of a hand from a man who didn't understand. The most traumatizing night of my life. My persona was altered through little fault of my own. Nobody will suffer from these events more than me. Creating a memory that would never fade. The slurping sound of the suction caused me to suck in my breath as I prayed to God to forgive me and asked Him to hold her in His arms.

I understand its stigma. Abortion isn't designed to be used as birth control. It isn't intended to erase a terrible decision. It was an option for a reason, though. I went to college without a second thought — and couldn't wait to do so — for the sole purpose of getting out of my house and away from the responsibilities I'd had no choice but to take on. I can say it erased nothing. The choice to abort stays with you for the entirety of your life. No matter what, that night, that party, that rape, and the resulting abortion is brought to mind whenever I hear the Beastie Boys. This is my proof that a sound can trigger such traumatic recollections. I would rather hate myself than hate my own child. A song brings back horrific memories. Could I look at her and not feel resentment? How fair would that be?

I think about her and who she would be. *A cute ice blonde, crystal blue-eyed girl who loves to dance. She'd like dresses: bubblegum pink. And twirling. Constantly. At parent-teacher conferences, we would discuss how to keep her in her seat because she always wanted to twirl. "Watch me!" she'd say in her choir voice as she'd twirl to make her dress swing. "It's quiet time, Olivia," the teacher would say, putting her finger to her lips signaling* shh. *She got her love of dancing from me.* Olivia means "the olive tree — a symbol of fruitfulness, beauty, and dignity." She is a part of me. I made her, even if I couldn't keep her. She is always twirling. She is my tiny dancer, and that song connects me with her. She is the memory I carry with me of a traumatic night, in the way I want to remember her. She understands.

Rob and I dated for two more months after this. He was sensitive and patient, but I didn't want to be touched in a sexual way at all. I didn't even want to be kissed. I wanted to be coddled. Once I started feeling better and moving past this, Rob stopped coddling me. I went in for a hug and was about to thank him for helping me get through this and for staying by my side, but he broke up with me on the spot. The only thing he couldn't forget was that "it could have been mine." He didn't understand. I didn't blame him; I still don't. I'm grateful he went through that with me.

As for the guys at the party, I never saw them again. Or if I did, I had no way of knowing. To this day, I hate the Beastie Boys.

CHAPTER THREE

Who Am I - *Age 19*

A year later, I hadn't seen Rob in months. He switched apartments at the end of the semester. Lying on Rachel's floor, flipping through the pages of the latest Cosmopolitan magazine, I heard my phone ring. It was a 941 area code. As I answered the phone and heard my name on the other end, my mind went blank. It was about my father. I couldn't speak.

"Ma'am, we need to know if you can come get your brothers temporarily or know where we can take them. They will be coming with us otherwise."

I gulped. *"Don't take them anywhere! I'm coming home and I'll take care of it."*

My father had relapsed. He'd started drinking again. One time. Once. This time, it nearly cost him everything. My daddy was a gunsmith. He loved guns. He liked to shoot them, clean them, take them apart and put them back together, buy them, sell them, and look at them. But when he started drinking, he liked to play with them. And not the way you play cards or sports. Dangerously. According to the sheriff's department, my father had gotten drunk because he was depressed. He'd had to file for bankruptcy and the only person who kept the household from falling apart had left for college. I felt completely at fault. I was 19 years old and stood for nothing.

He got depressed, drunk, and deranged. Waving a loaded gun around, he shot a few times through the ceiling, and then called the cops to come remove the boys so he could kill himself. Flabbergasted and completely devastated, I tried to pick up the pieces of my little brothers' broken hearts. I fought for them.

When I arrived home, a neighbor was sitting with the boys while Dad was at the hospital being Baker Acted. The Baker Act is a Florida law that is enacted when a person is exhibiting signs of a mental illness and is expected to cause imminent harm to themselves or others. It requires a minimum 72 hour hold at a psychiatric facility for immediate intervention and treatment. I'd made it home in record time — just in time to watch the boys being taken away.

"I'll take them," I pleaded with the investigators. But as a college kid with no job, no money, and technically no home, I had no choice but to let them go into the foster care system. As I sobbed uncontrollably, a social worker pried them out of my grasp. I felt like I was betraying them, but there was nothing I could do. They were crying simply because I was crying, and they had no idea what was happening. They were

11-year-old boys with no parents and a sister who could barely take care of herself. The worst part was, I wanted to be their mother, and I wasn't. I just wasn't.

Both boys looking back at me, one reaching out his hand to me, was more than I could bear. I blew them a kiss and fell to the ground, inconsolable. This lit a fire in me that could not be put out. I gave it all up. I dropped out of college and worked my fingers off to get them out of the system. I got visitation and could take them for one day. I felt shorted. I was not allowed overnights, or more than a typical eight-hour workday. Feeling like a criminal — though I hadn't done anything wrong — I tried to save them. I wanted them to see some good in the world when there was nothing but bad around us. We went to McDonalds or the zoo. I took them to the mall or to the park. We even went to the beach. Scared and helpless, I did my best to get them through it. But at the end of the day, I had to take them back. Like I was borrowing them. I cried the whole way from the door to my car. I sat and sobbed for a few minutes before I could drive away. Every time.

Parentification. Who's the adult here? Repeatedly asking my dad to confirm he would be home by 7AM so I could go to work. Sharing a vehicle, a gas tank, and child-rearing responsibilities. Connecting our pinkies, making him promise not to have a drink.

When I came home 30 minutes before curfew, I turned the volume down on the television and gently laid a blanket over my dad, who was snoring in the dreadful recliner. Peering in on the twins, I found one sprawled out on the floor over his cars, and the other hanging off the bed, feet dangling off the top bunk. I carefully situated and rearranged each so they were comfy and snug in their beds, gave them each a kiss on the cheek, and flipped on the nightlight before tiptoeing out, leaving the door ajar. I realized I could undoubtedly sneak in late, and no one would be the wiser.

When dad was out, I worried every second until I heard the blip of the car alarm signaling his safe arrival. The boys had gone fast to sleep hours earlier after warm baths and full bellies. The dishes were stacked neatly in the drying rack, and dad's clothes were lying out for him instead of in the dryer. That way, when he got home, he could mindlessly change into his sweatpants and compression socks before turning on a movie he wouldn't finish while polishing off a massive bowl of Butter Pecan ice cream and a gallon-sized jug of Diet Verners. I'd find these left on the floor for me to clean up in the morning. Blip blip. I had 32 seconds to turn off the TV and crawl into bed like I'd been there all night instead of waiting up for him before he walked in the door. Parentification at its finest. Who parented who?

When we had moved into this 4-bedroom house, we were broken. Devoid of emotion. We were coming out of a marriage with a stable mother figure and other siblings; a real family. It was the one thing missing from my life, thus far. I wanted it back. Disappointment and heartbreak were all I knew. Dad assured us this was better, and we were going to be okay. He was our only caretaker, so I went with it. At sixteen years old and as a sophomore in high school, this felt like starting over. Again. It's all I knew how to do. Start over. Getting established and growing roots was not something I was accustomed to. I was terrified of change. The unknown. Ironically, my whole life was one big change after another. I suppose I got used to it, or at least thought I did. "The woman of the house" was my new title. Cleaning, cooking, laundry... I did all of it. Dad worked late most nights, and then he was in school two nights a week trying to better himself, he'd say. When he was home, he was often so tired he slept in that ugly recliner he loved so much. It leaned back only 6 inches, and his feet would still be on the ground, but there was a permanent indent from his butt in the seat of the chair. He was married to that hideous thing. I once mentioned briefly that we should get new furniture, and he scoffed. My brothers were eight when we moved into this house. I was frequently in charge. They listened to me sometimes. When they didn't, they'll tell you I pinched them. Or sat on them. Once, I think I even locked them in their room until they promised to listen to me. But I loved them. I loved them like they were my own children. I fed them, bathed them, and put them to bed. I got them up in the morning and walked them to the bus stop a mile away at the end of our street. I was there when they got off the bus. It was me who struggled through their homework when they needed help. It was me who had to watch Barney on repeat for hours. It was me who got them dressed, tied their shoes, and kissed their booboos. It was me.

In high school, I never thought I would have a boy who liked me, let alone a serious relationship. I met Aaron during my freshman year when we lived on the same street. I admired him from afar. After an initial awkward conversation, the butterflies fluttered every time he said a simple "hi." I often stayed late after school for extracurriculars. One Thursday at school, I was dressed to the nines in a simple black-and-white dress I had dolled up with a shawl and some peep-toe shoes for a band concert that night. Not knowing anything about how hard my home life really was, Aaron asked, "Why are you so dressed up?" My thoughts and my words did not connect, and I seemed annoyed. This cute boy was talking to me and was interested in what I had to say.

"I have a band concert tonight."

"Tonight?" he asked quizzically.

"I won't be able to come home first." Not in the mood to elaborate, I shrugged.

"Oh, alright," he said, laughing.

Time stood still, and my heart skipped a beat. We talked at the bus stop almost every morning after that. I nonchalantly accepted his birthday party invitation the summer between ninth and tenth grade, which resulted in my first kiss when he walked me home after the party.

"My mom told me to walk you home," he'd said calmly. I was overjoyed that she did. Nothing has ever compared to that first kiss and the electricity that jolted through my body. I floated to my front door and didn't hear "how was it?" from my siblings. I lived at the end of the street, and he lived at the beginning of it. Taking a nightly fifteen-minute walk to see him for thirty seconds was the epitome of young love. Waiting for him at the end of his driveway to walk the additional 200 feet to the bus stop together was the highlight of my mornings. I never knew if he was as thrilled as I was to sync our steps, but in those few minutes, nothing else mattered. I felt seen, and I'd sought that feeling ever since. Shortly after we started dating, he moved. Then, we moved. I missed our morning and nightly meetups. I begged my dad for a phone in my room. I was needy, emotional, and hormonal, and he didn't know how to handle me.

"If you love me, you'll let me," I pouted with my bottom lip sticking out. The phone was installed that week. It led to hour-long phone conversations with Aaron well into the night. It was the only constant; he was the only positive at that time in my life, and I relished in it. I was ecstatic when he got a car. He drove me home from school when I didn't have practice. I think he even kept the green shorts I wore to practice. I kept a t-shirt of his almost every time I saw him. I traded it out for a new one that smelled like him.

As a band geek, music was my passion. I had practice three days a week and games on Fridays. I had hardly any social life outside of school, band, and my boyfriend. None of my friends had to take care of siblings. None of my friends had to make sure their parents got home okay. None of my friends had to alternate their teenage dream with the person responsible for their upbringing. Rotating nights off allowed me to feel somewhat normal. I landed a part-time job at my dentist's office every other Saturday morning, so when I came home, my dad would head out. When I got my job at TJ Maxx *as a sophomore, I had to humbly explain why I needed Saturday nights off, which was unheard of in retail.*

Unfortunately, I had to drop out of band my senior year, which was the best year for band. The boys used to go to an after-school program, but my inclination is that Dad could no longer afford it. I couldn't get to and from practices anymore because he got a second job, and I then had to get the boys from school, as well. It was devastating, but I took it with a smile. Without band, I no longer had to attend the football games, so I used my Friday nights to go on dates instead. It appeased me, but I sacrificed something I loved for those boys, who I loved even more. Aaron and I went to the movies quite a bit, but we rarely watched the movies. We christened places that shouldn't have been christened, but I was a teenager in love with no rules. At least I wasn't doing drugs, drinking, or stealing things like many other high schoolers I knew. In my mind, this was better. I was loved. Love was something I severely lacked, growing up. I was going to hold onto this as long as I could.

After high school, instead of planning for our future, Aaron joined the military. While he was in boot camp and basic training, we had no contact. I still had a year left of high school, and we tried to make it work. I felt deserted even though I knew it wasn't intentional. The heart and brain often speak very different languages, and I couldn't help how I felt. I was frequently told by members of both of our families that the love I felt for him wasn't real because I didn't understand what it meant to be in love. According to them, young love and the fairy tale we were living did not encapsulate real life. I knew he loved me. I also knew this was exactly what abandonment felt like. He said he loved me but left anyway. Just like my mother had. Just like everyone. It also reminded me of what believing I'm not enough felt like. If I'd been thinking clearly, I may have realized it was for the best. But I was too fixated on feeling left behind yet again. The feeling of not being enough was far too great. Eight weeks with no contact was hard for me. I had no sense of time, and everything felt intensely longer than it was. I had this preconceived notion in my head that I wasn't enough, and when he came home on a short visit, we were different. We had changed. I tried to make it work, but distance can either make the heart grow fonder or tear you apart. It did the latter. He tried so hard to help me understand, but I was in self-protect mode and I didn't listen. I couldn't hear anything except that he was leaving.

I worked two jobs my senior year of high school while still tending to my brothers. I used the extra money to help with household expenses. My dad bought the groceries, paid the mortgage, and covered all of the utilities. I contributed to the car payments, paid for my gas when I used the car, and paid the bill for the phone I had forced him to install in my room. We compromised, all while making sure my brothers knew they were loved. They were shy, scared, socially-anxious kids who just needed to be loved and cared for. I tried to ensure they were, with every ounce of my being. Their biggest hurdles were the stutters they worked endlessly to overcome, most likely instilled in them due to their frequent uprooting. I did my best to steer them in the right direction.

They became my entire world. I would not give up on them. I just wish they knew.

My brothers were fostered by several different people. A family friend of ours tried to take them for some normalcy. She was good for them, but the man she lived with was not. They were eventually taken out of that home and put into another. There were so many foster kids that my sweet, innocent, precious little brothers were neglected. Sharing a room with four other kids and sleeping on the floor, their only saving grace was that they were together. When they were removed from this home and placed into a third, I was torn. Torn between feeling grateful they were with a loving woman who nurtured them and feeling like I had abandoned them. They should have been with me. It took every ounce of my being to leave them at the end of the days I got to spend with them. They were my heart and soul. No decision I ever made excluded what was best for them.

Month after agonizing month, my dad fought to get the boys back. Countless counseling sessions, multiple AA meetings, numerous court hearings, and eventually, he won. They say alcoholism is a disease. I strongly disagree with that. I believe that alcoholism is a choice. An addiction, but a choice, nonetheless. A cancer patient can't just choose not to have cancer one day and get better. A dialysis patient can't just decide his kidneys are going to start working again. An alcoholic can choose not to pick up another drink and improve their quality of life. My father chose to put the bottle down. We had been down this road before, but when you've hit rock bottom, the only way to go is up. He enrolled in a rehab program, got accepted into a housing community for recovering addicts, and the boys went home almost a year later. Just like that, I was on my own again.

CHAPTER FOUR

The Cycle Begins - *Ages 20-21*

I went back to college life, but this time I had no plan. I wasn't even enrolled in the school anymore, and my scholarship had been revoked. Wing it. That's one thing my father had taught me. *"Never act like you don't have a clue. Wing it. Everything happens for a reason."* I can still hear his voice in my head. Even knowing I had no guidance after high school, and not quite sure how to transition from child/parent to individual, I winged it. I was on my own. I was off to a very rough start.

I had lost contact with Rachel when I went home, because my concern was for my family, and I hadn't called her, nor had she called me. I wondered often if she ever thought of me. I wished I had stayed in touch with her, because she must have moved at the end of the year. I'd assumed she would be in the same place or at least call me if she moved. Maybe she had horrible memories of that year and

I triggered some of it. I'll never know. New guys lived in Rob's apartment, and they said Rachel and Jake broke up months ago. They had heard she moved on campus to the dorms. I looked briefly, but I couldn't find her. You needed a key card to get into the dormitory hall. I pretended to be looking for one when a crying girl came running out. Her idiot boyfriend, or so I assumed, came running out behind her. *"Come back!"* he shouted. I grabbed the door and went in. A tall, pretty brunette was putting on an ugly tan Mary Jane. She was sporting a hideous cream-colored sweater vest with a blue ribbon tied at the shoulder. *"I didn't know he had a girlfriend."* She shrugged and searched for her other ugly shoe. I remember because I had accidentally kicked it as I walked in, and it flung under an ottoman in the hallway of the student lounge. The philanderer picked up books, blankets, and dirty clothes looking for it. There were eight dormitory halls in total. I quickly realized that I was in an upperclassmen hall, and I definitely did not look the part. I knew well enough that she wouldn't even glance my way, let alone listen to me if I tried to tell her where her shoe was. Her shoes were repulsive, anyway. I would be doing her a favor. I pointed, knowing she wouldn't see. I doubted Rachel would be in this hall. Not wanting to look obviously out of place, I perused the bulletin board. Books for sale. Roommate wanted. Study groups. Kappa Sigma party. I promised myself I would never attend another college party.

I had no business being on campus. I had no scheduled classes, nor any housing on or off campus. I should have met with the admissions office to get re-enrolled for the next semester. Instead, I found myself in the alley behind campus near fraternity row. I had literally no place else to be. A short, busty redhead came striding up beside me, her ponytail methodically swinging behind her. The neon yellow tank top she was wearing barely covered her chest, and her right butt cheek peeked out from under her white denim shorts. "PARTAY!" She screamed. Her breath smelled like chemicals. That bleachy hand sanitizer smell. Tequila. She was sipping from a campus cup holding something that obviously needed to be concealed. "Are you headed to Kap'?" She asked in a singsong voice with her head tilted the way a dog's would when it heard a sound across the room. Her colossal hoop earrings tickled her neck as she looked at me. I stifled a moan. I definitely did not want to hang out with a sorority girl.

"I'm not sure where I'm headed," I divulged.

Her demeanor changed. *"Come on. You can go with me. You look like you need a pick-me-up."* She handed me her secret cup. I was hesitant to take a drink from a stranger. The last time I trusted someone, I ended up with multiple heartbreaks. I knew you needed an invite to go to a frat party. She sensed my curiosity. *"Nick will let you in if you're with me."* She started to jog ahead of me. *"Come on!"*

Her name was Heather. She was a marketing major. Nick was a senior and well-known on the Kappa Sigma alpha chain. They hooked up on occasion, but they weren't dating. She was his booty call, and she seemed proud to be so. *"Beefcake"* she called him. *"You gotta get yourself one."* Nick was the epitome of college frat boy. Tall, tanned and muscular, with arms bigger than my head. With a square jaw, butt-chin, a smile that displayed his one-sided dimple, and crystal-clear baby blue eyes you'd swear sparkled when he winked at you, he was hypnotizing. I wasn't completely sure I wanted to be there, but I followed Heather anyway. She told me I could be anyone I wanted to be tonight, but I couldn't be underage. This was prestige. This was my "in." I wasn't technically a student anymore, but they didn't know that. I could be someone else and try to forget what led me here. *"I'll introduce you,"* she said as she grabbed my hand.

Nick greeted us at the door. *"Whoa! Who's your friend?"* Nick winked at me.

"Nick, Brittany. Brittany, my boy toy," she smirked.

"Liquor's in the kitchen, keg's out back." As she shimmied by him, he nipped her shoulder with his perfect white teeth.

"Marking his territory?" I furtively asked her.

"Shh. He's cute. It's ok." She still had a hold of my hand.

"Who's Brittany?" She put a finger to my lips.

"You are." She smirked and squeezed my hand.

I sat on the couch alone and was contemplating just sneaking out the side door when the music interrupted my thoughts. It was the song *"Hanging by a Moment"* by Lifehouse and the lyrics spoke to my thoughts in the present moment. This is all I know. Live in the moment. Nothing matters except right here, right now. You will never get this moment again. Soak it in.

"Drink?" I vaguely recall being asked as the red solo cup was held very close to my chin. Leaning back to see who was holding it, I heard Heather. She and Nick had disappeared for a while, and I had just realized that I lost track of time. I was hesitant to drink. I knew nobody else, but I gingerly held the cup with much reluctance. I loosened up, as Heather pointed out when she returned. I found a friend that day.

From that day forward, we were inseparable. I moved in with Heather the following semester and I registered for one class to attend campus events with her. We went everywhere together. Every study group, every student event. We ate breakfast, lunch, and dinner together. We attended every party together. She was my BFF. My gal pal. My person. This is what I thought college was truly about. Late night study sessions, early morning exams, football games, frat parties. I hadn't talked to my dad since I left the second time. Betrayed, hurt and confused, I couldn't fully grasp my feelings. All I could comprehend was anger. So when she asked me to go to Miami for spring break with her, I didn't say no. We spent the entire week on the beach: morning, noon and night. You can drive on the beach, drink on the beach, even sleep on the beach, which we did. I loved every second. On our last night there, I met a local. She invited us to her bungalow. I fell in lust with the scenery, the surroundings... and her roommate Kevin. He was charming. Not at all my type, and looking back, I never would have gone for a guy like him, but he overcompensated in the personality department. I laughed all night and couldn't wait to come back. I promised I would. I eagerly awaited the day I could get back to him, although I had no idea when that would be.

After that semester, Heather graduated. I had enough credits to transfer out, and although I told the admissions rep that's what I was doing, I didn't transfer anywhere. I needed a change. I was losing my sense of self. I had no money, and I wasn't sure when Heather was leaving. She was job-hunting, sending out her resumé to companies all over the country.

I had always been self-sufficient. I learned responsibility at a very young age. I grew up long before I should have, but I wasn't taught the proper skills to thrive in the real world. Although I spent more time taking care of the family than either parent had, there was still a parent around I was learning from. Even bad behaviors are learned. I had tried the "on my own" thing before but didn't feel equipped to take care of myself because I was constantly thinking of others' needs ahead of my own. I realized I was a codependent person and needed to cohabitate. That summer, I went home with Heather to Nashville. We visited her sister at the bar where she worked. We got clearance to roam the bar however we wanted, taking shots directly from the bottles, dancing on the bar, serving locals without measuring; tips started flying and drinks were slinging. We both acted as faux bartenders for three weeks. I became Brittany the cocktail waitress. I dyed my hair blonde and changed my wardrobe to low-cut tank tops and skin-tight jeans. I found a niche. We left with over $5,000 each.

We went back to Florida. In Miami, every week through March and April was spring break. We partied it up for a solid month. Every week saw an influx of new people. We rented an efficiency on the beach and started working as cocktail waitresses at a late-night club. We did everything together, including taking on stage names. I went back to the bungalow on the beach, but my crush had moved. Eventually, Heather got an irrefutable job offer as a party planner through a hotel in New York City. I couldn't go with her. This was her big break, and I would only be in the way. It was a mutual decision. Moving across the country was not an option for me. I needed to be able to get home to my brothers quickly if necessary. And without a job of my own, I would be a burden. She promised to call me every day. We were BFFs, after all. She called me when she arrived, but I never heard from her again. I was heartbroken. My person had left me again.

I kept the efficiency, the job, and the façade. I became Brittany and had a fake ID to prove it. Back when he and Heather were a unit, Nick had a buddy that made fake IDs. I tried to reject it, but nobody said no to Nick. *"We're just changing your birthday. It's still you."* I went with it, and Brittany was born. I was fascinated with becoming this new version of myself. Brittany could be anyone from anywhere. Her parents could be highly respected. Brittany could be who I wanted her to be. During spring break, the owner encouraged bikini tops as uniform. I made over $7,500 one weekend. Spring breakers were good tippers, and all I did was deliver drinks. I wondered if Heather would even know how to look me up. She only ever called me Brittany. I don't think I ever told her my real name. I worked in fancy night clubs and swanky bars. The girls that worked in these bars were a tight-knit group and I fit right in. We took some wild trips and did some crazy things, but I was enjoying this new life I had created. I felt a closeness to them in ways they never knew.

We all fell out of touch and went on with our busy lives, but that time meant a lot to me.

A few months later, the mysterious stranger walked back into my life. There's an old adage that says what doesn't kill you makes you stronger, and one that says everything happens for a reason. I can't say I wish I'd never met him, but I do wish I didn't have blinders on. I recognized the man sitting at the bar and tried not to run towards him. *"Hey stranger,"* I said with a smirk. He looked over his shoulder with the mischievous grin I remembered all too well. He hugged me a little too tightly. *"Ain't you a sight for sore eyes. How long have you been back?"* I never would have gone for a guy with poor grammar, but he had this mesmerizing aura that pulled me in. I told him I went looking for him and he told me a long, drawn-out story of how he and his roommate had a falling out, and he moved out. He walked me home that night and said he thought about me every single day I was gone. I felt wanted, and it was what I'd been missing. He wasn't the man of my dreams, but I couldn't detach from his magnetizing spell. He quickly became obsessed. Within weeks, I had to quit my job because he didn't want me waiting on other men, and I certainly couldn't be seen in public with a bikini top on. I moved in with him because he had to spend every second with me. It happened fast. I was pregnant within three months, married within six. I wanted my child to have what I never had: two parents; a family. I wanted this baby. I felt that I was responsible for something again. Taking care of someone fulfilled my sense of purpose. But I also felt trapped. Kevin went to every doctor's appointment with me. He went to the grocery store with me. He went to the bathroom with me.

When I took a shower, he would sit on the side of the tub and talk to me the whole time. He became controlling and dominant. I wasn't allowed to have any friends.

I tried to leave twice. The first time, I was a few months pregnant. The morning sickness lasted all day, and I was exhausted. The sound of glass breaking in another room woke me up. As soon as my eyes opened, the nausea hit me again. I meandered out of the bedroom for some ginger ale and crackers. I walked into the living room to see ten strangers sitting in a circle passing a pipe. He looked up and saw me standing there, and he demanded I go back to my room.

"I need—" I started to say.

"I will come and get you when I'm finished," he said through gritted teeth. He talked to me like I was a child and I had misbehaved by coming out of my room without permission. I was mortified. I returned to my room and started packing my bags. I could raise this baby on my own. A few short minutes later, he came into the room, threw my bag in the hallway, and pushed me down on the bed.

"You aren't going anywhere." I asked for some ginger ale, and all I got was *"In a minute."* He tossed a bucket into the room and locked the door from the outside. Like I was a prisoner. I tried to open the window, but he had sealed it down somehow. *When did he do that?* I thought about breaking the window, but he would hear and stop me before I could get one leg out the window. Eventually I fell back asleep, and when I woke up, the door was open.

The second time I tried to leave, Kevin slammed my hand in the door and pushed me to the ground. I fell on my stomach. He had been on a six-day bender and hadn't slept. I begged to see a doctor to make sure I hadn't hurt the baby. He insisted on going with me, and he spoke for me. *"She fell,"* he said. I was moving too fast, and I fell. That was his story. The baby was fine, and I hugged the doctor. Kevin promised the doctor I would never be left alone again, and I would be glued to his side for the remainder of the pregnancy. I fought back the tears. The doctor must have sensed a problem because a social worker showed up at my door soon after the appointment. She just wanted to talk about my injury, but I shushed her and pleaded with her to go away. I lied and said it was a salesman. Kevin must've suspected something because he made me change doctors after that. I told the office my insurance changed and the doctor wasn't covered on my new plan. She never questioned it. For once, I wished I wasn't invisible.

I wanted this baby before, but now, I wanted her more than ever. I was completely alone in the world, and I needed her. She saved my life. She was everything I didn't know I needed. Kevin was addicted to the high that cocaine and wreaking havoc brought him. When I told him I was pregnant, he was ecstatic, and my freedom immediately vanished. After broken promises to take care of me, he was permitted to party all night, every night with anyone willing, but I wasn't allowed to be seen with another person of any gender. A walk through the neighborhood incited the third degree. A casual chat with a neighbor caused an uproar. He was convinced I was having an affair with the woman I spent hours with at the pool. How did I miss this? Depression is the social death penalty. I didn't want to see daylight. I didn't want anyone to see me with him. I didn't want anyone to see what I had turned into, who I had become. I never left the house. Even if I wanted to, I had to write down exactly where I was going, what I was getting, and when I would return. If I came home with one less or one more item than I wrote down, or if I was a minute longer than expected, I received a verbal beatdown that disheveled my self-worth. I cowered. I trembled at the sound of his voice. I cringed at his touch. I crumbled. I cried myself to sleep every night. I was in my own torture chamber. He reminded me on a daily basis that he owned me. I was his possession. I couldn't speak unless spoken to. I wanted out so much that I was almost ready to end it. End everything. I definitely did not want to live this way. If I weren't pregnant, I may have tried something. But, as I was sobbing, her tiny foot kicked me in the ribs, and I wanted nothing more than to hold her in my arms. She saved me and I vowed to show her she was worth it.

Chloe was born six weeks early. I was so grateful that Kevin missed the birth. I don't know where he was, but I didn't care as long as he wasn't there. I begged to be let out of the hospital early. I was going to take my baby and run away with her, but she was too early. She wasn't swallowing, and her lungs weren't very strong. She needed to be in the NICU to let her lungs develop a bit longer. She had a feeding tube and an IV in her hand. My life was completely different. My life belonged to her. She was my saving grace. She was what I needed. I stayed with her in the hospital every second of every day. On day two of being in the NICU, one of the nurses was changing her IV from her tiny hand to her head, and she started crying. I couldn't hold her, I couldn't touch her, and I cried right along with her. Another nurse put a tiny Tigger in her tiny hand, and she gripped onto it. Her hands were covered in mittens, boards, and wires; she couldn't get them into her mouth. But she never loosened her grip on that tiny Tigger. The day we were released from the hospital, Kevin was there to take us home. I just wanted to take my daughter home and then I would figure out the rest. In the parking lot, that day we headed home, she dropped the Tigger. We got an orange kitten and I named it Tigger. Two weeks later, he told us we were moving. *"Just get in the car."* We drove for three days and arrived on the west coast. He claimed he got a job, but I never saw him leave the house. I certainly couldn't, so I would have noticed.

Things got much worse. Breastfeeding didn't work, and my supply was too low to feed her. That was depressing enough. *"You are useless to her."* I felt discouraged and worthless. He threw a sugar jar at my head, hit my thigh with a full water bottle so hard there was a welt for a month, and smashed my hand with a hot frying pan. But becoming a mother changed me from the inside. Sometimes, you just have to fight. I fought silently, though. I had to beat him at his own game. I begged him to let me go visit my dad. He had a granddaughter, and if I didn't let him see her, he would come looking for her. Grandparent's rights. I winged it. I promised I would only be gone for a few days. His "supply" was running low, so I told him we wouldn't be in the way if he wanted to refill it while we were gone. I promised him, pleaded with him, that things would be different when we returned. He hesitantly let us go with a threat. If we didn't come home, he would come find me, and then I'd never be seen again — but he would tell my father where he could find my dismembered body parts.

I called my dad from the airport. I hadn't spoken to him in nearly two years. Without hesitating or asking any questions, he assured me he would be there to pick us up in four hours. And he was. I had nothing but my daughter and the clothes we were wearing. He hugged me and took us in like no time had passed at all. When I left home before, I was a child. Now, I had one. He didn't say anything about the baby in my arms. He just took her from me, let me collapse into his arms as I sobbed with relief, and took us home. He never asked me a single question.

He lived in a tiny two-bedroom apartment that he was leasing through his program — a subdivision for recovering addicts and the homeless. He had cleaned up his act, he was working, and my brothers were thriving. He was a success story. There was no room for us, but he gave my daughter and I his bedroom since he still had the revolting recliner he slept in. I was grateful, and I found a deeper appreciation for that chair. Some things change, but some things never do. A parent's love is unconditional, and I learned it that day, because, yet again, I chose to go back to my dad, which was a better solution than returning to Oregon.

As for my promise, I broke it. I changed my phone number and promptly served Kevin with a restraining order. We never went back. I held my infant daughter in my arms and suddenly understood the love between a mother and a child. I protected her from evil, and she saved my life. She was my missing puzzle piece and I started living my entire life for her. I published my divorce in the newspaper. That whirlwind relationship lasted a total of eighteen months. I'd like to say the first one doesn't count, but you can't learn from mistakes if you never make any. I can't say I wish I'd never met him, because then I wouldn't have my little Rory — that's a *Gilmore Girls* reference; if you haven't seen it, you should — but I could've gone a different direction entirely. I might have saved myself some heartbreak. I was smarter than that, but I let my severe need for affection cause a lapse in judgment.

CHAPTER FIVE

Mommy Issues - *Ages 11-13*

The woman with the eyes that reached the deepest part of my heart brought me into this world, and all I ever wanted was her acceptance, her love, her unconditional, devoted, undying affection. She saw me as a burden for reasons I will never know. I felt like an inconvenience. She tried to love me, or so she claims, but her efforts were weak at best. The foundation on which I stood was shaky. She saw through me. She never saw me. She never heard me. She never understood me. I was a child in the fight of my life, and she ignored me. Her undoing was her own fault. My undoing was her fault. The woman with the half-smile I wanted to replicate exuded strength I wanted to emulate. She showed warmth to everyone but me. Her hollow stare bored through the pith of my innocence. The woman knocked me off my pedestal. The woman who had protected me had suddenly become my enemy. And it was only just beginning. She liked to say I was a "big girl." I promised myself I would become that.

No matter how old you get, there will never be a time when you don't need your mother. I learned that the hard way. I grew up many years without mine. We had our differences and we believed different things. She chose a different priority from being my mother, and I'm thankful I didn't turn out to be distraught and troublesome. I'm certain the other female figures in my life helped guide me in the right direction. When I was young, I remember good times with my mom. We would read together. She read me a story nearly every night. The same book: *The Pokey Little Puppy*. I just know it was about a curious puppy that went up a hill. I enjoyed that time with her and loved when I could read it back to her word-for-word and how proud she was of me. She thought it was just from memory, but when she spelled out words to her friends to have an adult conversation without me knowing, I said the word aloud. Although I didn't understand the meaning of the words, her adult conversations started happening in other rooms. I was smart – too smart for my own good. She knew that. I got that from her. She was my idol when I was young. I wanted to be just like her. She worked hard but still wanted me around. She was a nurse at a nursing home, and I went with her on occasion. I would color and make rounds to visit all the old folks; I had a bunch of grandparents. They loved me, and I enjoyed all the candy they gave me. I wanted to be a paramedic until my favorite old guy died and was taken away by one. I cried my little eyes out and didn't want to be a paramedic anymore. My mother was also protective. When the little girl down the street beat me with a jump rope, leaving welts all across my back, my mother marched down there and demanded an explanation and an apology. I don't remember why she hit me with a jump rope, but I remember my mom yelling at her with her hand in mine the whole time. I remember the hamster I sat on and how its eyeball popped out. I remember the dolls I got for Christmas one year, and refusing to go anywhere without them. I remember visiting "up north" and the extended family was there. I was the only child of the family, and I secretly loved all the attention. I remember a rocking horse and a pet turtle that was left out in the sun too long. I remember being tricked into eating liver, and I remember falling off my mom's bed and hitting my temple on the corner of her dresser. I remember walking to and from school and the little old lady that gave us cookies in the afternoon. I remember my address and phone number for the first house I lived in. I remember all of these things because I was with my mother. I remember when my twin brothers were born and the loudspeaker announcement that was heard in my second-grade class. I was taking a timed test, and I was almost done with it, which was a rarity. The whole class started cheering and it embarrassed me. Crying with my head in my arms on my desk, I smeared the answers on my paper. My dad picked me up to go to the hospital and I remember seeing the boys in my mom's arms. I begged her to give them back. I pushed their bassinets out of the room and told the nurse to take them away. She was *my* mom. They couldn't have her. I was an only child for eight years. Now, I had to share her with TWO boys. I didn't like them at all, at first.

My childhood was not like everyone else's. I'd like to say I was a happy child despite this, but the truth is, I had a cracked foundation at best. It was only a matter of time until I shattered. I had a dream. Every little girl had a dream of growing up, getting married, and being a princess. I wanted to be a princess. A dancing princess. I made up songs and lyrics and danced around the living room with a pillowcase on my head, in the back yard with a pinecone wreath, or in the bathroom with a towel cape. Dancing was my escape from the constant noise. The bickering, the yelling, the fighting. With an imagination that could reach the stars, I envisioned the world at my fingertips. A bright and bubbly girl with blue eyes that shined when I dreamed, or so I was told: *"What are you thinking about? Your eyes are shining."* I would get lost in my thoughts, often envisioning a life free from pain; away from the yelling, the fighting, the cursing. I was a small girl with big dreams. My parents were toxic to each other, to themselves, and to me. Their poison seeped through my porous mind. From a young age, I was subjected to pain, anger and hatred. It's a wonder I turned out ok at all. Maybe I wasn't ok. Maybe I wouldn't ever be ok. If only I knew how true this statement would be. But I danced anyway. When I didn't know how to cope or how to feel, I just danced.

No one knows her like I do. She lays silent and still in the dead of night. Her mind prances to the darkest place of the imagination. The ballroom of her sanity sashays effervescently through the confines of her imagination. There is no place like it. It takes her down a torturous road. The 'what if's and 'could have's permeate her being. I could walk that road alone, or I could embrace it. They say silence is golden. For us, silence is the song. With no music but the beat inside our hearts, we find our own rhythm. As she glides across the rink of her inner melodic symphony, I find my peace. Music has never betrayed me. Songs speak to my emotions. Skipping one that doesn't resonate or replaying one that relates is the simplest path to joy. The misery of her lonely company has called her. I feel her bubbling over with sorrow. The heaviness of the weight on her shoulders is overpowering. She is fighting not to fall to her knees in defeat, fighting to carry the burdens and crawl if she must. I feel her. I see her. I try to take some of the burden, but she digs her claws in, grits her teeth, and pushes through the treacherous mountain that is standing before her. She doesn't know how hard this road is going to be. She just knows she must keep going. I'm unsure why she feels this way, but I watch in awe as she faces this alone. I reach out my hand, but she pretends not to see me. I am invisible. She is intangible. Her demons try to infiltrate her innocence. Instead of succumbing to their power, her own song writes itself. The beauty that is unbeknownst to her is coming into its own. She dances. She twirls. I sway. She is me.

The twins' cribs were in the corner of the living room because we were in a two-bedroom duplex. My dad was drunk all the time. I vaguely remember him hitting my mom with the phone. He took her by the hair and threw her against the wall. I vividly remember my dad getting taken out on a stretcher because of alcohol poisoning. My brothers were crying, my mom was packing, and I was scared. The next thing I knew, we were moving. Over and over and over again. I'm not sure if my dad found us or if my mom just liked moving. I was losing her, and I knew it. She wasn't home as much. I couldn't go to work with her anymore, and she was depressed. A new man was in our lives and she wasn't my mom anymore. The man was not pleasant to be around. He gave me lots of unwanted attention. He was verbally abusive. As I was developing and transforming, I was sexualized and violated, yet I still stayed on the straight and narrow. I tried to talk to my mom about what was happening to me, and she turned me away. She refused to believe anything I said. She demoralized me and told me I was being defiant and unruly. My brothers and I became tight-knit. We clung together. I was eleven and they were three. I succumbed to their demands to watch Barney on repeat. I made macaroni and cheese for breakfast. I locked myself in the closet to escape, but I quickly got attached to those two boys that looked alike. She threatened to call my father and said I could go live with him. I begged her to do just that. I hadn't seen my father in three years. The last time I saw him, he was being taken away by ambulance. I didn't know him. I still felt safer going there with him than staying in my current situation. My mother must have known where he was the entire time, because she made a call and I was on the next flight out. I immediately felt relief and guilt at the same time. My brothers were being left behind, but at least I wouldn't be degraded anymore.

Moving in with my dad was bittersweet. Again, I didn't really know him at this point, so I was standoffish and shy. This whole thing had happened so fast I didn't have time to process it. My dad had remarried to a woman who had three kids of her own. What if I wasn't wanted? I couldn't have withstood being rejected by both parents, but my father welcomed me with open arms. I was skittish, but I finally felt relaxed.

Three years went by before I talked openly about the abuse. It dragged on for three more agonizing years before it was finally just put away. I've survived so much already, why would this be any different? If my own mother didn't believe me, why would a stranger? I was out of the situation, and in every sense, I was left alone.

All of that prepared me in a proverbial sense for this next chapter.

CHAPTER SIX

The Cycle Continues - *Age 24*

I'd already gotten out of an abusive relationship; how in the world did I get myself into another one? Live and learn? Apparently not me. I knew the signs, I knew the red flags, but I ignored them. That intuition, gut feeling, sense of danger... mine was broken.

He looked at me like I had longed for someone to look at me. With want, need, and desire. But I was usually wrong. My guilt-ridden instinct had led me astray and the lack of direction I exhibited made me doubt myself. I mistook obsession for love. He wanted me in his gluttonous way and not in the way of my quiet demeanor. I begged to be seen like I had been only one other time. Typically, I blend in with the background, never being the center of attention. I just wanted to be seen, noticed, understood. His eyes bored into mine and I was entranced. The coldness in his heart, the darkness in his eyes, and the weakness in his self-control was titillating and it gave me chills, but not the good kind. It was new to me, and

I lapped it up right out of the palm of his hand. My brilliant, open mind enveloped the uneasiness I felt, but I ignored it. He was charming, and he had reached right into my chest and ripped my heart out. Easily influenced, I longed for love, true love, the kind that quieted the stars, the kind that opened up the depths of a hardened heart, the kind that I had experienced only once before, thus far. Hurt, heartache and pain were the only things I'd ever felt. "Everybody leaves" was my motto. I still don't fully trust anyone. Having zero desire to ever be hurt again, I put up a wall. Growing up without much guidance, I was taught to self-protect. Guard your heart and trust your intuition. *"You've got a good head on your shoulders"* was ingrained in my brain. I ignored every red flag waving in my face, and it destroyed me.

I dreaded the sound of his truck pulling into the driveway, the gravel popping under the heavy tires, the roar of the engine as it neared the house, the vibration of the motor as it slowed to a stop in front of the garage, the tire tracks slightly askew as they settled into their place in the grass, the hiss as the motor quieted when the key turned it off, and the crunch of the gravel beneath his feet as he stumbled toward my safe haven. It was only safe as long as he wasn't in it. There was something ominous in the air as I waited for the door to open. The next few hours depended on how this went. Was the house clean enough? Were the kids quiet enough? Was the food cooked enough? Was the laundry done? The dishes? He would quickly scan the kitchen, as it was the first visual he would judge the day on, and my attitude would change. The creaky front door should've been fixed months before, but it was my alarm. It gave me a few seconds to determine how the rest of the night would go. He would trod a heavy-footed path to the bedroom with footsteps that sounded like stomps. It had been a hard day, but I couldn't be caught sitting down or taking a rest. To feed, bathe, clothe, and entertain the children wasn't work, according to him. Hard labor and heavy lifting were work. Cleaning was nearly impossible, and if I managed it, it was never good enough. Working with an infant attached to the breast, a clingy toddler attached to the leg, and an emotionally-needy child attached to the heartstrings was inconceivable. More often than not, the occupancy was staged to prevent an encounter. It was more trouble to avoid the impending doom than to accept it. His sigh made my bones hurt. I could decipher the sigh like a mother knows her baby's cry and could determine if he was hurt, tired, hungry, needed a change, or just needed a snuggle. Was he disappointed? Angry? Did he need his fix? I could only assume. I acted accordingly. It was exhausting to always be on the defense. Making chicken nuggets again because it was all I could manage, and the kids would eat them, I could already hear the venom spewing from his crooked mouth. I was a disappointment. Lazy, inattentive, and half-hearted because a more complex meal eluded me. The 2AM feedings for the baby went unnoticed. The 4AM wake up calls from the toddler who went to bed at 7PM because he refused to nap went unheard by my partner. The 7AM bus to school went unmentioned. The work I had to get done from 10-12 every day seemed unimportant. The nap I couldn't take without missing the 3PM pick up from school went unseen. The chaos that would ensue if I left Chloe alone with the boys was incomprehensible to him. The 5PM dinner preparation went unappreciated. The 7PM clean-up I did alone was undetectable. The 12AM bedtime I finally managed was unfathomable because of my wifely duties to the man of the house who expected me to oblige. Unimportant, unseen, unheard, unnoticed, unloved. This became my routine, a merry-go-round. I wanted off, but I got used to being dizzy. I memorized the sigh at the end of the workday and the once-over of the kitchen. I can still feel the fear that enveloped me each time he came home. There would be one of two scenarios: the thump of his steel-toed boot as it hit the ground and the release of the breath I didn't even know I was holding, or the click of the cap as it unscrewed from the neck of the cheap vodka he'd been hiding in the pocket of his cargo pants accompanied by the deep inhale of breath I'd been saving. The silence was deafening and the moment between the creak of the door and either of those sounds lasted an eternity.

The thump. When the door creaked and his boot thudded, it was going to be a decent night. He wouldn't be able to go the whole night without a drink, but at least I would get a few hours of the "good." He was understanding and kind, and the compliments were flowing. I was "beautiful" and "irresistible," and he was considerate and loving. This was the kind of attention and devotion I pined for. All was forgotten in those moments. Everything was okay, just as I'd suspected. Reaching up to put a glass in the cupboard, I would be caught off-guard by his bear hug. A fleeting sense of fear coursed through my body as my muscles tensed in anticipation, but I forced myself to relax as he laid his head on my shoulder.

"You're pretty," he would say in a childlike tone. Thank goodness for mascara and the clean shirt I had managed to put on.

"Good day at work?" I murmured.

"Mmmm," he purred in my ear.

Chills swept over the nape of my neck as he turned me around to face him. I leaned into his lips as he whispered in my ear words I'd only heard on Cinemax. As I kissed him delicately, pain seared into my ribs as he pinned me against the handle of the silverware drawer, ravaging my mouth. It was nice to be desired, and this was how I'd imagined a marriage would be: the lust, the desire, the raw attraction to your spouse. I couldn't comprehend that this was so far from the truth.

The click. With the click of a cap, I knew I had to be "on." I had to say just the right thing at just the right time. I had to know when to ask how his day went and how to be supportive and understanding. I had to know when to be seen and not heard. I would know what kind of mood he was in based on the position of his tires in the driveway and his boots by the door. I would inhale, tears welling. I fought to keep them from falling. The sting of his hand to my cheek was unforgettable. The forced smile and fake happiness consumed me. For a brief moment, I envisioned a deserted island where no one could hurt me. No one could leave, because there was no place to go. I imagined a life free of control and defeat. The memories of my childhood trauma flooded back with every raised hand, every loud voice, and every venomous word. I remember when my childhood was the worst I'd ever endured, having a father who enjoyed the bottle more than his family and another man who treated me like an object and turned my mother against me. Wanting to go back there was disheartening.

There were two completely different versions of the man I thought I knew. A Dr. Jekyll and a Mr. Hyde. I knew which version I would get by a sound. Throughout those times, I relied on my hearing more than any other sense. The sound of the cap. The sigh. The door as it opened. The pop of a tab on a beer can. The words that echoed in my head reminded me that I was a failure. The controlling mind games drove me into a repetitive sequence of insanity. I was expected to perform. To act. To be the perfect housewife as I was always falling apart. I couldn't show any weakness. I believed my weakness proved I couldn't handle motherhood and my kids would get taken away from me.

"You're such a slob. Can't you brush your hair and put on a clean shirt, for crying out loud?"

Unbeknownst to him, I had changed my shirt four times that day. As I had rushed all the kids out the door for the bus, I had chugged my coffee, and it had dribbled down my chin onto my shirt.

I never claimed to be a Miss Suzy Homemaker. I certainly wasn't a neat-freak, but I wasn't a slob. Organized mess, I called it. Having children meant I sacrificed a tidy home, but it was at least orderly.

"Ugh," I had huffed and tried to soak it up with the paper towels stuffed in the glovebox. That only made it worse. Change #1. I put a black t-shirt on. Can't see coffee on a black shirt. I was so sleep-deprived that I forgot the baby was colicky, and when I picked him up, he spit up on my shoulder and all down the front of my black shirt. Well, you can see white liquid on a black shirt, but I couldn't put him down long enough to change my shirt again, because he wouldn't stop crying if I tried. He finally calmed down long enough to sit in the swing, but if I stopped moving it with my foot, he wailed.

"Hey buddy," I cooed to my toddler. *"Can you bring mommy a shirt from that laundry basket?"* He put down his frog and toddled to the stack of clothes folded in the basket. I grimaced as he picked the one in the middle. I'll put those away later, I told myself. Change #2. My son handed me a red

scoop-neck tee with flounce sleeves. It's more of a girls'-night-out shirt, but it'll do.

After hours of rocking, Liam finally fell asleep. I put both boys down for a nap and refolded the laundry. The phone rang and I leapt to answer it before it woke them up. My neighbor wanted to borrow some milk. *"I haven't made it to the store yet."* Then we talked about the garage sale she wanted to have next weekend and whether I could help her. *"I'll let you know."* I hadn't realized I had sat down on the couch to talk to her, but I must have drifted off. I woke up with a jolt when a car alarm went off across the street. With a yawn, I stood up and stretched. I decided I should eat. I took my time making a sandwich, putting each dish in the sink as I used it, but I recognized I should have made it faster when I heard Noah say *"mama."* I had seconds to eat it before he would screech and wake up Liam, so I scarfed the sandwich down and groaned as the mustard oozed out of the bottom and dripped onto my red shirt. I grabbed another shirt from the basket and watched the pile of re-folded laundry fall to the floor as I fought back tears and got my son. Change #3 was a yellow shirt with flowers on it. It has buttons, which I appreciate when the baby wakes up to eat. With SpongeBob on the television, or "Bob Bob" as he called it, Noah plopped down on his blankie with his one-eyed frog while I made him a grilled cheese with the crust cut off. Since he was entertained and the baby was still sleeping, I started a load of laundry. Between the 3 shirts and the bibs and towels used to clean the spit-up, it was a whole load. As I folded the first load of laundry for the third time, creating piles on the table to be put away, Chloe burst through the door in tears, covered with bloody scrapes.

"What happened?!"

"I was running home and I fell. AAAHHHHH, OUCHIE!" her high-pitched screech pierced my ear.

"Ok, ok, ok. It's ok," I said as I scooped her up and set her on the counter.

She had scraped her knee and her elbow. After some TLC and the placement of a few Care Bears band-aids, she went outside to ride her bike. As I lifted two of the piles of laundry to put them away, I noticed the blood on my hand, which I had transferred to my shirt.

Hanging my head, I chose the first shirt I had in my hand. Change #4 was a green muscle tank. *"Whatever, at this point. It's a clean, dry shirt."* Then, just as he was pulling into the driveway and I was rushing dishes into the dishwasher, the water splashed across the counter and soaked my fourth shirt that day. The verbal thrashing I always got for my disheveled appearance echoed in my tired head.

"Are you too lazy to even change your clothes? You couldn't even do laundry?" he'd hiss at me. I realized that, yet again, the clean laundry was sprawled out across the kitchen table, with some falling to the floor. I knew I shouldn't dare try to explain it.

Yet, he would have claimed I did nothing all day if I looked presentable because I took the time to do my hair and makeup. He would have said I must have been trying to impress somebody else. Nothing I did was enough. I was always a failure, and no matter how hard I tried, it was never good enough. I was defeated and completely broken, and this was only one day. This mental abuse devoured my soul and my eternal well-being. When I bared my supple neck just to keep my hair from sticking to my sweaty skin, he interpreted it as an invitation. I certainly didn't feel sexy, and he only told me I was sexy for his benefit.

My husband's brief exhaled sigh was an attention-seeking sigh. I had no say in what happened next, not a word until that bottle was gone. My oblivion would dissipate. Suddenly, I was aware of everything I did and everything I didn't do. All people have bad days, and most would talk about them to relieve the stressors. I believed I was my own stressor, though. Perfection was my unattainable goal, and nothing I did was good enough. Dinner wasn't hot. My hair was messy. My clothes were dirty. The kitchen wasn't clean. The bed wasn't made. I didn't greet him at the door. He made sure I knew it. My visions of marriage, motherhood and happiness were tarnished. All I had ever wanted was to be a wife and a mother. My dream of perpetual bliss was forsaken. This was my reality, and it was my living nightmare.

CHAPTER SEVEN

My Living Nightmare - *Age 22*

It wasn't always this way. Raising my brothers in my early years had equipped me with the tools I needed to grow into a self-sufficient, self-reliant and independent woman. After suffering through decades of loss, heartbreak, pain, and betrayal, I was determined to persist. I was pursuing a law degree, and I was completely focused on myself. I had already lost this dream once. Feeling wanted once before had resulted in a demeaning falsehood that gave me Chloe; the only good thing to come of it. Escaping that nightmare and escaping Kevin was the hardest thing I'd had to do at that point in my life. I had virtually no understanding of the real world, let alone how to survive in it, but when you comprehend that another human life is now your responsibility, you find strength and courage you never knew you had. I was better than what I had been through. I'd learned that if I wasn't happy, something needed to change. I was already a survivor, a leader, a mother. I was determined to make the most of it. I wouldn't get caught up again. Big dreams for a little girl; that was always the vision. My eyes were shining when I picked up and walked out that day, hell-bent on starting over and making a name for myself, and with the greatest human being to ever grace my life — the little girl who depended on me to make a difference — I vowed this would never happen again.

Dan was charming when I met him. He caught me off guard. I forgot myself in his blonde hair, eyes that changed color, and the way one side of his lips turned up into a crooked smile that made my heart race. Everything instilled in me up to this point vanished. The sound of his honeyed, gravelly voice bellowing my name seared through me. Glancing over my shoulder, I sucked in a breath and it caught in my throat. His charismatic and captivating ruggedness drew me in. It never occurred to me how crazy it was that he changed his schedule so he could run into me. His charm, appeal, and magnetism enthralled me. Mesmerized, I agreed to a date.

The first time he called without having asked me for my phone number should have been red flag number one. We had gone to the same gym for years. I'd never seen him, but I wasn't going to the gym looking for a husband. It was the only place I could shed the unwanted weight the unkind world had placed on my shoulders. In my short 22 years of life, I had begun carrying thousands of pounds of pain, guilt, and despair that shackled me to a lifetime of defeat.

As much as he was starving for attention, I was hungrier. Disregarding the stirring in my belly that something wasn't right, I fell. I saw the passion in his eyes. The longing, the hunger, the craving for my touch. The warmth of my kiss engulfed him, and he saw the desire slowly enveloping my soul. The ease at which I melted his heart... it all came so naturally. The passionate, zealous obsession of it made him weak in the knees and faint-hearted. My embrace eased his pain and grief. At one time, we had it all. He was falling, and I reached for his hand and took the plunge.

Very quickly, I got caught in his snare. I can't explain the hypnotic manner with which he reeled me in. He tossed me up on a pedestal that consumed me. Never had I felt so riveted, and I wanted more. I had hidden my deepest desire in a sacred place, but it was being drawn out of me, and I couldn't stop it. I was in a trance when I was with him. As a single, working mother, I had very little free time. Visiting my father and spending time with my brothers or my friends occupied most of that time, and he escaped my thoughts while doing so, but one call from Dan unraveled my plans. My world revolved around him. The more time I spent with him, the less I saw of my family and friends. I relished the fact that he wanted me. His vows and promises oozed into the slivers of my fractured heart, and I leaped right into his web.

"I can't get enough of you," he whispered through gritted teeth. *"Just stay."* The tiny hairs on the back of my neck stood up, but I believed it could have been from his intoxicatingly smoldering blue eyes staring intently into mine. The angle of his head, the crooked smile, and the voracious power of his mouth as it engulfed mine made my world go dark. With one flick of his tongue and one spark in his eye, I melted and the light inside me burned out. I just didn't realize it until it was far too late.

He was attentive, complimentary, and sweet. He always pulled my chair out for me, opened my car door, and offered his coat. I always walked on the inside, slept away from the door, and never paid on a date. He was the perfect guy... until he wasn't.

His web of deceit was revealed later. The truth had been bent so much and the lies had been retold so many times that he believed them, and I questioned the truth. I wondered if I had gone crazy. Why didn't I remember the stories the way he was telling them? *"Right?"* he would look to me for confirmation. All I did was nod.

My suggestions became his ideas. His recommendations became enforceable. He convinced me to change my hair. Unluckily for him, I loved it. It gave me the power to see my self-worth. Taking my role as a wife seriously, I defended him often. I frequently apologized on his behalf. I spent more time explaining how what he said wasn't what he meant than I spent speaking for myself. Friends came and went. The longer I stayed with him, the smaller my circle became. I accepted the blame when plans fell through. He told me I was the problem.

"You should have put your hair up." "I told you not to wear that." "If only you were more pleasant." I felt those words in my core. Attacking my character was the most effective way to manipulate me, and he knew how to do it. If I'd been perceptive enough to realize my biggest lie was pretending everything was okay, I would have been compelled to save myself. My greatest weakness was him. I was powerless to see through his façade. I truly believed that loving him would fix him. Ever since I was a little girl, I always dreamed bigger than what was possible.

I lived at the edge of despair for years. He thought "diapers" was a code word for cheating. Going to the store was a luxury. I felt like a prisoner in my own home. I'd had more freedom as a teenager than in his home – my own personal hell. I told myself this had to be what love was. From my mother to my childhood abuser, from my daughter's father to this, I knew no better. Acceptance is the final stage of grief, and I had been grieving my entire life. I believed it didn't get better than this. Dropping the "love" bomb in our first month together should have been the second red flag, but my skewed perception of love told me he was Prince Charming. In that first year, I changed my wardrobe, my way of thinking, and my last name. I felt needed. Nearly nine months to the day, we had our first son. I'm fairly certain he knew when I conceived, which prompted the marriage proposal. Looking back, I was a pawn in a game of chess I didn't even know I was playing. He sacrificed the queen so his self-righteous ego could volley with the knight. The knight, for him, was everything but himself. Suddenly, my dream of becoming a lawyer was awash.

I defended him with every ounce of my being. What I saw was not what I believed. He was funny and sweet with a dimple that puddled me. His hypnotic, sultry image melted my already buttery exterior and turned me to putty. I saw the best in people, and I truly believed he was a knight in shining armor with a sword that penetrated my aura and left a void he claimed only he could fill.

Then he saw the fire in my eyes. They burned through him like a stake through the heart. The hatred, the anger, the resentment. It ripped at his core, making the world feel as if it was crashing down on him in one sudden attack. Love: it's a curse. It's fake. It's warped. The twisted, evil malevolence of it made him weak in the knees in a new way. This time, he reached for my hand, but he just kept reaching.

He never really swept me off my feet, only pulled the rug out from under me, like when you fall off the swing or trip over a board and fall on your back and the wind gets knocked out of you. It's those long, agonizing few minutes when you can't breathe, can't speak, can't move. My entire marriage was like that. The wind was knocked out of me, and I fought to find my voice, my breath again. It happened so fast; I never saw it coming. He swung the pendulum in front of my face long enough for me to see the swirls and the haze completely overtook my sense of balance. I faltered, and he swooped in and knocked me off my feet. Not in the head-over-heels kind of way. He was like a devil in disguise. He was my monster under the bed, but he never bared his teeth. He just dug his claws in, and no matter how hard I shook, I couldn't get them out. He was hooked, and I was stuck.

CHAPTER EIGHT

My "Safe" Place - *Age 5*

The only familiarity I had with alcohol was my understanding of my father's addiction. The brain has a fascinating way of blocking out traumatic experiences. I indistinctly remembered my dad passing out most nights with a multitude of half-empty containers of liquor strewn about the floor. Sometimes I would accidentally kick one across the room, its "liquid gold" pooling around my dad, and my horrified hand would fly up to my mouth in anguish, hoping it didn't wake him up. I had vague memories of my dad hitting my mom with the phone because she poured his gin down the sink, and when he started yelling, she picked up the phone to call... someone. I heard stories of my dad putting sloe gin in my sippy cup of orange juice so I would "take a nice nap."

Then there was the disturbing memory of the tattoo:

I won Around the World in school. I was never any good at math, so I was excited to go home and tell my parents. My prize was a temporary tattoo that peels off onto your skin with water, and I put it on in the bathroom before I walked home. A few weeks prior, there had been a news story about "bad guys" lacing those tattoos with LSD. My dad had been drinking since noon the day I got mine. When I showed him my arm, he freaked out. Incorrectly assuming I was trying to get high in Kindergarten, he called me a name that wasn't mine. I didn't even get to tell him how I won it. The smile slowly faded from my face, and I dropped my head, dragging my feet to my room. Later that night, as my father was slurring his words trying to make his point, and my mother was pleading with him, I inadvertently got in the middle of their fight. He grabbed my left arm and I flew. The horror on my mother's face was etched in my mind.

"Leave her alone." That's the memory that repeated in my head. "Leave her alone." I froze. Time completely stood still. Running to my room, tears freely falling, I slammed my door. My Strawberry Shortcake pillowcase covered my face, and I only wanted to fall asleep and for this to be over. He barged into my room and pinned my arm against the wall.

"If I ever see this again, I will break your f—ing arm." When he left my room, I crawled out the window and hid in the U-shaped shrub in the front yard. I called it the girl tunnel. I stayed there until my mother came out and brought me back inside.

"You're a big girl," she said.

I moved in with my father when I was eleven years old after sexual abuse and impurities nobody believed happened while living with my mother. The last time I had seen my father, he was being taken away by ambulance with alcohol poisoning. Tears streamed down my face as I was yanked away from my childhood home where I had lain with my mother as she cried herself to sleep; where I had prepared numerous bottles to feed my infant brothers, and where I had snuck out the window to hide in the "bush fort," the U-shaped shrubbery in the front yard which became my safe place. Instead of a beach or the mountains or some other place people usually go to in their minds when they need an escape from trauma, I go back to being five years old in my bush fort.

My protector. Greener than any other bush in the yard, the petite violet flowers beckoned me among the emerald leaves. The shrub was my blanket as I hugged my knees to my chest. The wind whistled through the leaves but never reached the far-left corner where I had curled up. I rocked back and forth in my leafy rocking chair, and it consoled me. The sun couldn't touch me, making it seem darker than it was. That shrub shielded me more than any person could. My protector. My bush fort. My safe place.

Twenty-eight years later, I still heard my father's threat in my nightmares. The pain of re-living that memory worsened after meeting the man my father eventually became. He had no recollection of it, as is to be expected. He didn't remember much of my childhood; I wish I didn't either. But in that small time frame, when my father had threatened to break my arm, my tiny, imaginative world was harshly brought back to reality.

These were my early memories pertaining to alcohol. I wanted nothing to do with it. After the college party I wished to forget, alcohol was the devil, and I vowed to banish it at all costs.

Paradoxically, at 22, my first date with Dan involved boxed wine. Walking into an impeccable apartment with nothing out of place, I let my guard down. The walls I had built too high for anyone to climb suddenly became shaky. As the door opened, I crumbled and turned to putty. He knew what to say and how to say it. Charm was his *modus operandi*. He winked and his eyes sparkled. His dimple radiated a beaming smile. Weak in the knees, I would have said yes to anything. As he handed me a glass, I suddenly forgot about everything I hated. He was an addictive, tantalizing, delicious poison. He said all the right things and picked up on every one of my weaknesses, and I succumbed to his sexual magnetism on our very first date.

After the break-up with Aaron — the only man who had made me feel anything but disappointment up to that point — I was learning how to open my heart again. I thought nobody could ever compare to him. At that time in my life, Aaron was the one, and I was struggling to get over him. Having grown up in a motherless home and rediscovered my inner beauty that wasn't objectified by every man I had encountered before then, Aaron was the only one who had truly seen the depths of my soul. When we parted ways, I felt unloved, unwanted, and unworthy of anything. After the college party, I was a shell of myself, devoid of human emotion. When anyone gave me any kind of attention, I relished in it. I soaked it in like a dehydrated soul thirsting for the basic human needs of love and acceptance. I lost my self-respect. Sex meant nothing. Love meant nothing. Feelings were incomprehensible and lust was at the forefront. Simply being "wanted" was enough. Whether I was considered attractive or sought after was a second thought. I yearned for attention, affection and the greatest in the hierarchy of human needs, love. I insatiably desired it, so when I got a taste of what I longed for, my depravity consumed me and every sense of normalcy escaped. I hungered for that satiety and hunted it. The basic human need for love overtook everything else, and I internalized it.

Shutting down everything I knew, I converted into a shell of a human, but Dan made me feel something that kept me coming back for more.

Something about Dan was magnetizing. An invisible force drew me to him. The way he drew circles in the palm of my hand and the way he ran his hands through my hair and let it fall from his fingertips was comforting. As I rested my head on his shoulder, I exhaled. I felt safe for the first time in a long time. I saw his upturned half-smile in my peripheral vision. The Cheshire cat grin. He knew what he was doing, and I did not. He was my new bush fort, and I clung to him for dear life.

CHAPTER NINE

My First Heartbreak - *Age 6*

While my father was out drinking for days on end and my mom worked, I would walk myself 10 blocks straight to school with no stops. Every morning, the Brady Bunch would let me know when to leave for school. I watched one episode every morning. Cindy, the youngest, was my favorite. She was the one vying for the most attention, the one who was often left out. I attempted to put my hair in pigtails like hers once, but I couldn't get my hands that high up on my head. My tongue danced across my bottom lip and the corner of my eye turned up when I was concentrating. My fingers worked tirelessly to gather all of my platinum blonde hair and when it would fall and graze my shoulders, I would sigh from the side of my upturned lip and give up. Even at six years old, I understood defeat.

On the way home from school, I would stop at Ms. Molly's house for a warm chocolate chip cookie every afternoon. She was nice. Her white hair was always up in a perfectly coiffed bun and she wore shoulder pads that made her arms look tiny. I always giggled. She'd pinch my cheek and say, "See you tomorrow dollface." She made me feel happy. Ms. Molly was one of my fondest childhood memories.

My house was small and usually empty. On the wall behind the brown splotchy couch was the giant swordfish my dad caught during a guys' fishing trip in Key West. Its mouth hung open and I stared at it. The razor-sharp teeth that edged the long, pointy nose glistened as the light from the living room window shone in. I imagined being a fish and being free, swimming and having the whole ocean at my beck and call. With my signature shrug, I pulled my bean bag out from the corner and plopped down to watch Mr. Rogers Neighborhood like I did every afternoon.

This had been the routine every day since the first day of Kindergarten. I would skip down the road, pretending I was just like every other girl; yet, my life was vastly different. I felt frequently alone. On the weekends, when I would go to work with my mom, the residents would grovel over the little freckle-faced blonde with a smile that lit up the room. My snaggle "vampire" tooth was my trademark. I secretly liked going. Everyone always told jokes and I felt special when I was allowed to feed the residents. They would tell me they could always hear me coming; they heard my little girl giggles as I danced down the hallway to the beat of my own drum. My jelly shoes would click and clack all the way to the rooms. I would get candy making rounds with my mom, and it was the highlight of my day. I would bound into the room, skipping one foot in front of the other with a chocolate in my palm. I hadn't realized how much pure joy I felt at that place. Little did I know, the day I saw my favorite old guy being taken away with his face covered, my tiny heartbroken soul would never be the same. I waited many painstakingly long minutes for him to pop out of the sheet, but he never did. This was pure love at its finest, and the kind of love I sought after ever since, though I didn't know it. My very first heartbreak.

CHAPTER TEN

Rising - *Age 25, ages 11-16*

Dan picked up on my need to be wanted; only I needed to be wanted in a different way. My inhibitions escaped me and I longed for attention. He drew me in like a vampire who needed blood, a demon who needed a soul, a parasite who needed a host, a fish who needed water. My oblivion wore rose-colored glasses. I pined for acceptance and approval so much that I ignored the alarms sounding in my soul and tolerated the eventual mistreatment.

My "mommy issues" were much deeper than my "daddy issues." Without being taught by example, I knew nothing about being a woman, let alone a mother. A mother is one who gives birth to a child and brings them up with care and affection. By default, my mother had been the sole provider of my upbringing, and she had failed miserably. I idolized her, but I didn't feel she ever chose me. She never fought for me. She never protected me. She never acknowledged me in any regard. As a mother, I can only hope my daughter grows up to be a better version of me as I teach her to improve where I was lacking. I just wanted my mother to love me. All my life, I fought for her affection and felt disregarded. I like to believe she tried, but sometimes I didn't know if she cared at all.

Nothing should come before your children. You don't even come before your children. I don't think my mom saw that manual, the one that tells you "How to be a Good Mother." There is only one chapter: Choose your child. Always. Period. End of story. Children know no other way than what their mothers have shown them. By disregarding me and dismissing any thought I brought to her, all she taught me was that I didn't matter. What a distorted, unfair self-image she handed to me on a silver platter. I. DON'T. MATTER. The fact that I didn't end up in jail, or on the streets, or on drugs, still amazes me today. When your own mother — the person who brought you into this world — wishes you were anywhere other than in the same room with her, it changes you. It hardens you. It makes you question your very existence. At least, that was the effect it had on me.

At eleven years old, the lesser of two evils was moving across the country to live with my dad instead of remaining where I felt stuck. Years had passed, and I had no idea what I was getting into, but anything was better than where I was coming from. I was pleasantly surprised to find my dad was a different man. A better man. I immediately felt relief and guilt at the same time. My brothers were being left behind with the mother who I felt had abandoned me.

I didn't really know my dad at that point, so I was standoffish and shy. This whole thing had happened so fast; I didn't even have time to process it. I couldn't help but wonder, what if I wasn't wanted? I couldn't have withstood being rejected by both parents.

My father welcomed me with open arms. Our relationship intensified as I got older. I only had a few good years with him, and it wasn't nearly enough, but he saved me in another way. I went into his home with a guarded heart, a cautious awareness, and a shielded self-worth, praying I could find peace within my soul. Wise beyond my years through no fault of my own, I became painfully aware of my surroundings. Self-protection, self-preservation, and self-defense were vital to prevent self-destruction. I built an iron-clad suit of armor. If rejection from my own mom didn't extinguish my will to live, I could persevere. I could persist. Not only could I survive, but I could thrive. Not realizing I was about to break the cycle, I fought. I put on the cape and armor, and I marched forward as every tear I could ever cry fell at my feet. Dejected, rejected, and with a fire in my belly, I was destined and determined to be a phoenix, to rise from the ashes of this scorched and blistered path. I was about to change my story; I just didn't know it yet.

I once saw an anonymous quote that said, "If you don't know your own worth and value, don't expect anyone else to calculate it for you." You will ALWAYS be undervalued. Your value appreciates each day you fight for yourself. Appreciates! It's taken me decades to realize this: I get better with age. My value appreciates. Whether you appreciate me or not makes no difference. Your opinion of me is either right or wrong. There is no in-between.

As a teenage girl, sitting on the doorstep waiting for my mother to visit me, the repetitious feelings of disappointment and rejection were like nothing I'd ever felt. My mother never came. She didn't choose me. The realization that she would never choose me was a stake through the heart. It defined everything I would believe about loyalty—or the lack thereof—betrayal, and loss. Hardened and untrusting, the core of my existence was frayed. One flimsy pull, and I'd shrivel at the seams.

Unwanted, I can tell you with certainty, is the worst feeling in the world. All I wanted was to be acknowledged. Seen, heard, and shown that I mattered. Whether anyone knew or not, whether anyone believed me or not, whether anyone cared or not, whether anyone understood or not is irrelevant. I simply wanted acknowledgement that it happened, that I exist and that it matters. Whether the incident lasted minutes or years, whether it was seconds ago or decades ago, it still happened. My feelings matter. My truth matters. My emotions matter. Excuses don't. It mattered then and it matters now. I matter and so do you. Never let anyone undermine your existence. I did it for far too long, and it was emotionally devastating. The basic needs of survival are food, water, and shelter. The basic needs of thriving are acceptance, love, and acknowledgment. I simply wanted to be acknowledged.

CHAPTER ELEVEN

The First Blow - *Age 26*

My sheltered sense of security was a fallacy, and my vision of protection was disrupted. I didn't recognize that Dan was alluring and entrancing only when he was drinking. I also didn't detect that I was captivating and enthralling only after a fifth. I liked him that way, but I didn't realize what made him that way. I wanted to be needed so desperately that I missed the signs, the hints, the suggestions. I relished in being enticing to him. My biggest weakness was my own insecurity. Every person up to this point in my life had disappointed me, disregarded me, and discarded me. So full of love that I couldn't give away, my tarnished idea of happiness overwhelmed me. With a thirst for acceptance and an insatiable hunger for love, rationality and equanimity eluded me. With each step, I fell further and deeper into his twisted web of pretense and hypocrisy, and I lost myself. I forgot everything I stood for, and again, my dreams were remiss.

Domestic violence is never an isolated event; there is always a second time. His charming, carefree persona camouflaged his predatory, possessive nature. Once it happens, it will happen again. It becomes second nature. It becomes routine. It becomes easy. Never in my lifetime did I believe I would be a statistic. Never did I imagine my husband, the man I loved with everything I had, the one person who stood next to me and vowed not to hurt me, would leave the biggest scars. The first time he hit me was a blow literally and figuratively.

Late on a Friday night, the kids were in bed, and I was cleaning up the kitchen. He was drunker than I'd ever seen him, falling down, slurring, swaying as if on a boat in the middle of the ocean. We only had beer in the fridge, and he'd been home for several hours. He was drinking something else, but I didn't know what or how. Where had he gotten it? I scanned the kitchen and the dining room and glanced into the trash can as I hurriedly threw away the scraps left over from the kids' dinner, but I found no evidence of anything other than six beer cans. He could function after drinking a six-pack. Increasingly frustrated, I watched him in my peripheral vision, trying to find an excuse for his behavior. If I hadn't seen a belligerent drunk before, I may not have known what I was witnessing. The occasional binge was probably not cause for concern. I made a mental note to see if this happens again. I wouldn't bring it up; I shook it off. I planned to finish the dishes and go to bed. I yawned. Then, he pinched me hard on the butt cheek that was peeking out of my sleep shorts. I jerked away, slamming my knee into the cupboard in the process. If he was flirting, it didn't usually hurt. Giving him the benefit of the doubt, I thought, *maybe he doesn't know his own strength right now. His inhibitions are gone. His clarity is fuzzy. His lucidity is unintelligible.* Either way, I was not in the mood for playfulness or anything else. Pinching me there was a summons. A literal booty call. I definitely was not in the mood for that.

"OUCH!" I said a little louder than I intended.

"Whaa-" he slurred.

"Just go to bed," I said as calmly as I could muster.

"Come with me," he garbled.

"I want to finish cleaning this up and then I'll be in." I was praying he would be fast asleep before I got there.

"Since when do you clean?"

Slamming my closed fist down on the faucet to shut the water off, I turned around to face him. *"Don't do that."* I said with a furrowed frown.

"Shuddup," he murmured almost incoherently.

"Do not tell me to shut up." I enunciated that sentence. I got bold. *"Go. To. Bed."* I was less calm as I turned him towards the bedroom. He grabbed onto my arm, and I escorted him down the hall towards our room. Almost there. He slid his hand up my leg into the bottom of my shorts, and I swatted it away. *"NO! Just go to bed."*

"Whore." He said, more brazen and articulate than he'd been for the last several hours. I never understood his reasoning for calling me names like that. I wasn't sure he even knew what that was. Wasn't I acting the exact opposite of that? Words that attacked my character set me off. I can only assume he knew that, because if I didn't react, he would continue spewing words at me until I snapped. A negative

reaction was better than no reaction to him. As I pleaded with him to be quiet so as not to wake the kids, he put his finger to my lips a bit harder than I appreciated. My upper lip pinched between his finger and my front tooth. I jerked my head back more forcefully than I intended and gingerly touched my tongue to the inner fleshy part of my lip. His knee-jerk reaction left a bruise on my cheek. The solid sound of his fist to my cheek bone was forever embedded into my memory. A soft thud with throbbing pain immediately following. The door to the garage was not latched, so when I slammed into it, I lost my footing on the step down and landed on my back. The hot tears streamed from my swollen eye, but not out of pain or fear. I was completely mortified. Nothing shocked me anymore, but this... this was appalling.

"Did you..." I started to scream and then whispered, *"just hit me?!?!"* I remember screaming, and then immediately hissing that sentence to him because the kids were sleeping. They were always at the forefront of my mind. Always. He hiccupped. He sat on the couch and within milliseconds, he was out cold. I didn't dare look in the mirror. I went to bed holding a bag of frozen peas to my face. This was not happening. It wouldn't happen again. He would be sure of it. I would be sure of it. Part of me knew I was wrong, but I didn't know how wrong.

Every day felt like I was walking across a glass floor with a crack down the middle. With each step, the crack was getting longer and wider. One wrong move, and the floor would collapse underneath me. Only, he was the crack in the floor. With the eggshells snapping under my feet as I walked, the blisters just kept forming. If I only... if I just... if I... I was under constant scrutiny from myself. If I would have kept my mouth shut. If I would have just let him talk and defame my character, and not tried to defend myself, he might not have escalated. If anyone knows how to de-escalate, it's me. If anyone has a thick skin and can take verbal slander, I can. I let a swarm of actions just roll off my shoulders, but I could not just let "slob," "lazy," or the "c"-word go.

CHAPTER TWELVE

What He Still Holds Against Me - *Age 28*

Healthy relationships include time away from each other. Girls' nights out — whether they're wild and include shots of tequila or quiet and include chick flicks and ice cream — are vital to self-preservation. We aren't destined to live life alone. Having friends is imperative to maintaining sanity. With the best of intentions, these nights away from responsibilities should have no repercussions. He needed every ounce of my attention, which I happily obliged, and I gave every percent of my effort. My only job was to appease him, maintain "trophy wife" status and raise well-mannered children who say please, thank you, yes ma'am, no sir, and excuse me. Children who didn't talk back, scream, or cry at inopportune times. Children who ate every bite on their plate, washed their own dishes, went to private school, and obeyed commands. And met other ridiculous, unattainable expectations. Stand by your man even to a fault. This was instilled in me by every woman I had ever encountered. I blamed that on my mother. No matter what he does; good, bad or indifferent; stand by your man. He supports you, so you hang on his arm and be proud. Be proud that he chose you because he can have any woman he wants, and you are the lucky one. Lucky me... and lucky for every other woman who wouldn't endure his wrath. The very few times I went out with my friends, it was like a furlough from prison.

Postpartum depression hit me severely. I already felt isolated and alone. Moving to the central part of the state to be closer to his family was exactly what I needed. However, the second we left the familiar safety net of my prominent family and friends, and those who supported me, I was tossed into my personal jail, and he held the key. We went out infrequently, and every time included alcohol. It was never just a casual drink with dinner; it was repeated shots of bottom-of-the-barrel gut rot, the kind that got the job done, the kind you drink just to get drunk and not to enjoy it or each other. I drank to tolerate him. He drank to tolerate himself. It was an endless cycle of vicious exploitation. I was used to dulling my pain with it, to try to be completely bereft of any emotion or sensation. The insulting insolence he vocalized to dethrone me from the pedestal he purposely put me on, hurt a little less when I numbed myself.

A rare, spontaneous date night started out pleasant. He was generous, romantic, and affectionate. Holding my hand all night, random 'I love you's with no expectations, and overall adoration for me was welcomed. Drinks with dinner should be savored and enjoyed. I can drink wine at home; with my expensive steak dinner, I wanted a Captain and Coke. Just one to partake on a random night out as I was trying to feel connected. My drink gave him the green light to get a shot and a beer. Then, another of both. I could sense the change in him but was enjoying date night. We ended up at a local bar. He took two shots for each round I had. Playing pool and picking out songs on the jukebox, I felt connected to him in a way I wasn't used to. I was dancing and shimmying up against him; he was flirtatious and playful. He was fun and friendly and affable. A couple of guys near us were playing darts rambunctiously. One of them came up to the bar and bumped into me.

"Oof. So sorry," he said with his hands over his chest.

My drunken companion chimed in. *"Nah, you should see these."* He pointed at my chest. *"I bump into them all the time."*

He went off towards the back of the bar to use the restroom and the guys were suddenly interested in conversing with me. I felt a headache coming on and wanted to keep it at bay. When I had worked at the bar in Miami, we kept pain reliever behind the bar. Rubbing my temples, I timidly asked the bartender, *"Do you have Advil back there?"* She didn't, but a passing patron offered me some.

"He said you were going to show me something," the guy smirked.

Drunk and with a pounding head, I lifted my shirt. A crowd gathered as my husband returned, seeing a stranger place two blue pills (Advil) in my hand.

"You were right," the stranger said, clapping him on the back.

The guy winked at me as he walked away. I saw the glare in Dan's eye as he grabbed me by the wrist. Confused, I hurriedly threw $20 on the bar counter as he walked me out the door. He held the events of that night over my head. He didn't remember the conversation leading up to the moment I bared my breasts, only that I did it. Yet again, I was at fault. I couldn't win for the life of me.

Bored with me only a couple of years into our already messy marriage, Dan claimed that we needed to spice it up. After I had been completely candid about my past and the manner in which I attempted to avoid rejection, he used it to proverbially knock me down. I was always accused of cheating or wanting to, yet he brought other women into our relationship, claiming it was to appease me. The worst thing about it was that I believed he did it for me. I truly felt this was the best way to "keep him." One of those girls eventually became a very good friend of mine. We talked and hung out often, and she quickly turned into my person. As most mentally healthy people do in emotionally healthy relationships, she recognized the need for time apart to rejuvenate, refresh, and regroup. I had forgotten what it felt like to be a woman and not a slave to my husband, my children, my home. She took me out one night to just be a girl. It was one of the most fun nights I'd had in an eternity. She convinced me to let loose and have a good time.

"Pretend you're with me." She winked at me. *"It'll get you free drinks, but not hit on."* It wasn't hard to fake, so I went with it. I didn't feel guilty about the innocent flirting. Instead, I dreaded the impending argument and verbal onslaught that would certainly ensue as a result of my "whorish behavior."

I sat alone in my car in the parking lot until I was able to drive home. Ever since I was a little girl with two other people to take care of, I put my needs last. I never worried about myself, and I consistently considered everyone else first. I had small children at home. I refused to risk getting a DUI or ending up in an accident, harming myself or someone else. So I waited. I waited a long time until I was okay to drive. This was before cell phones were a necessity and before ride-sharing programs could drive you home and go back for your car the next day. Yet, my choice to be responsible that night led to the beginning of the untrusting, unkind, and unnecessary behavior. Ten years later, he still firmly believes I cheated on him that night. The one other night he has to hold against me. His black cloud, if you will.

Every time I got a phone call, an instant message on the computer, a Facebook message, or even a smile from a random stranger, he was convinced I was having an affair. It was exhausting to defend myself every day. I stopped going out. I stopped talking to anybody. I stopped living to appease him, to assure him I wasn't cheating. I lost friends. I lost family. I lost myself. I lost everything, and it still wasn't enough for him.

I've always been timid, shy and completely non-confrontational. Attacking my character has always been a hot button for me. My "good" list of first times evoked pleasant memories, but Dan invoked horrible recollections and a "bad" list of firsts. The first time I stood up to him. My first black eye. His first foot in the face. The first time I realized my knight in shining armor was actually a devil in disguise.

CHAPTER THIRTEEN

Pain Like I Never Knew It - *Age 25*

Empty, half-empty, and sometimes still-full liquor bottles were regularly strewn across the floor. I picked them up and shoved them into the bottom cabinet where the cleaning supplies went. When I opened the top cabinet to get a baby bottle, a barren decanter fell to the floor. Audibly grunting, I turned just in time to see Liam put the lip of it in his mouth. I yanked it from his hand, wiped his mouth with the towel, and threw the bottle in the trash, infuriated. Digging through the diaper bag to find a burp cloth and pulling out a beer can, I realized Dan was running out of hiding places for the evidence of his alcoholism. Yet, I defended him. I made excuses for him. I covered up for him, and I even took the blame for him.

I was always very graceful. I was in gymnastics and dance growing up, so I rarely tripped over my own feet. I "became" klutzy so I would have an excuse for the bruises, the fat lips, and the marks. I blamed my klutziness. *"Oh this?"*

I'd say, noting the purplish bruise on my thigh. *"I ran into the table." "That? I tripped over the carpet and hit the doorknob,"* I'd say as I was rubbing the knot on my forehead. You can't help someone who doesn't want to help themselves. I wasn't ready to admit defeat. I loved him so much that I hated myself. I hated who I had become. I hated my life. I resented him, but at the same time, I loved him. How is that even possible? How can you love someone so much, and dislike someone considerably at the same time? Love shouldn't hurt. Love should not hurt. I wish I would've taken my own advice back then, but my blinders were on so tight, I couldn't see anything except my own faults. If you're loved, you feel safe and like you're wrapped in a warm blanket all the time. I, on the other hand, felt like I was left on a cold concrete sidewalk most of the time. It was the hardest thing I've ever done. He treated everyone with respect and kindness and love. Everyone except me, the mother of his children. How? How did I ever look into his eyes and fall so hard? Who had I become?

With the click of the cap, I realized I was holding my shirt so tight that my white knuckles were sore, and my fingernails were digging into my palms from gripping the spoon too long as I stirred the sauce on the stove. Would he be overly affectionate this evening? Or would he be unjustifiably angry? My every move, every word, every breath would be scrutinized. My eyes burned as I fought back the tears. He kissed the top of my head. I grimaced. I hated that. I still do. The booze wafted off his breath and I struggled gruelingly not to flinch. The forced smile I spread across my face between gritted teeth was my only saving grace. Any ounce of fear, anger, or sadness would be what my father warned me about. "Give you something to cry about," he'd say. As the sauce bubbled up and splattered onto my shirt, I stifled a whimper.

He believed not having a clean shirt was the epitome of laziness. This was only the beginning.

I would wake up with him inside me. I was his wife, after all. My body parts were his, and I had no control of them. This was marriage. I had to give in on a whim. No foreplay, no warming up; when he was ready, I had to be. Even at 3:45 in the morning with the promise of only fifteen minutes of deep sleep before a 4AM feeding, I wasn't allowed to not be in the mood. Even if I pretended to sleep through it, my body reacted whether I wanted it to or not, and he paid no attention. I was there and could lie there without any interaction, movement, or any indication of pleasure, and it didn't matter. As a tear landed on my cheek, I drifted off to sleep again, my underwear still bunched up and pushed aside, only to be awakened by the screaming infant who also wanted to mangle my breast. Only his request was life-sustaining and not soul-draining. And if Liam needed me, my husband didn't. I fell asleep holding the baby night after night.

CHAPTER FOURTEEN

Reflection - *Age 40*

Looking in the mirror now, I've done well for myself, considering my past. I was often jealous of others who grew up with two parents — normal parents — those who were given everything they needed and almost everything they wanted. If it weren't for two women in my life that gave a damn, I'm unsure who I would be now. Strength was not instilled in me. I didn't know how I was surviving. I don't know how much I believe in fate or circumstance, but I do believe everything happens for a reason and that the plan for your life is set out before you begin the journey. My voyage was not smooth sailing, but I stayed the course. I'm not without my flaws; I am nowhere near perfect. I'm sufficient at best, but I am me. And there's nobody else I would rather be. I've tried. I've attempted to be somebody else. Somebody who had it more together; more pristine; uncorrupted; undamaged. I pretended to be another person for several years, and it only taught me to appreciate who I really am, because that girl is enough. She didn't survive everything she had so far in life to break down now. I was going to be somebody. I was going to prove my worth. I will be who I am meant to be. Although I didn't come out unscathed, I prevailed. Behind a damaged smile, I stare at my reflection. I see resilience, potential, and determination. I also see sadness, hurt, deep-seated pain, resentment, and dejection. But I will never show that. I am putting back together the broken smile piece by piece as it still slowly crumbles all around me. One piece goes back on as three others fall off. Crawling my way out of the dungeon of desolation I found myself in, step by vigorous step, clawing with ragged fingernails chipping away even further as I dug in, I could see the path to my own redemption. And I was going to get there.

They see strength, perseverance, and tenacity. They see the drive, the effortless empathy, and the affection. I exude affection because I long for it so deeply. Growing up, I was led to believe that you get what you give. Yet, I was loving, kind, nice, friendly, trusting, thoughtful, and compassionate, and all I got in return was pain, hurt and heartache. I coveted human interaction profoundly. The gentle touch. The soft words. The loving embrace. The friendly smile. The engaging conversation. The feeling of community. That's all I craved. The aching need to feel wanted. To be seen. To belong. I often wonder what people see when they tell me I'm strong, or I'm triumphant, or unflappable. What appearance was I giving off? I was one trauma away from completely self-destructing, yet I'm still standing. What's meant to break you will only break you if you let it. It can also make you stronger and show you who you really are and what you're made of.

The internal battle is a back-and-forth dilemma of who I really am. Where I came from, though, was an uphill battle.

I lived a hard-knock life. Not the on-the-streets kind, but I knew despair, neglect, abandonment, betrayal and heartbreak. I fought to overcome it all, and I have the scars to prove it. The person looking back at me is a fighter, a girl who sees the best in people. The girl who seemingly brought out the worst in others, who summoned the malevolent tyrant others couldn't see. I was always the one not believed, the one looked down on because she was weak. Amidst all of this, I got my power back. The woman looking back at me was about to find out who she really was.

CHAPTER FIFTEEN

A Tiger Doesn't Change Its Stripes - *Age 23*

We went out infrequently. Some of the time, that was because there were three young children at home. More of the time, it was because he couldn't control himself. One drink turned into five. Five turned into ten. I was timid, quiet and tolerant. I defended him. "We don't get out much," "He works hard," "He deserves to let loose once in a while." If it had truly only been 'once in a while,' it might not have been frowned upon. His reason to go out was so that he could be expected to drink heavily, when in actuality his excuse to drink at all was because he was awake. His drinking escalated over the course of a year. I ignored it. I often drank to tolerate him. However, it was called "liquid courage" for a reason. My nerve to talk back, or defend myself, or finally call him out was the catalyst to the physical abuse, but this was years after the mental, emotional, and financial abuse had already begun.

I'm needy. I've always been that way. I've been self-sufficient and self-reliant my entire life, but with that, many basic human needs get overlooked. I need love. I need comfort. And, most importantly, I need attention. I was not a perfect wife. I never claimed to be Miss Suzy Homemaker. I was supportive and understanding to the best of my ability. I was also abiding and submissive to a fault. But, even if I was perfect, it still wouldn't have been enough. Even bad attention is still attention. My insatiable appetite for undivided attention was my biggest weakness.

Like the dark-colored stressed chameleon on the end of the branch, lying in wait until the threat of danger passed, I adjusted, blending into my surroundings. I changed myself to be as unnoticed as possible until the threat disappeared. Never feeling completely safe, I transformed. I lost myself and never really got me back. I camouflaged myself to become undetectable. With disheveled, unwashed hair and monotonous feelings of insignificance, I adapted. At church, at school drop-offs, at family gatherings, I plastered a smile on my face. Making myself look as put-together as I could, knowing he would be the kindest, funniest, most approachable man in the place, I buried the pain and changed the color of my skin to cope. However, a tiger can't change its stripes no matter how hard he tries.

Every extra penny we had went to booze. I got extensions on bills, paid just enough to keep the utilities on, received late notices, and bought enough food to keep us alive, but there was always booze. Always. Empty beer cans littered the floor of the garage next to the enormous garbage cans that were just emptied the day before. Finished pints of cheap vodka were strewn around the house, falling out of the cabinets, pouring out of the drawers, and tumbling out from under the bed.

A predator lies in wait before pouncing. A shark erupts from the dark waters below. You don't see it until it rips your face off. The lies that I was never going to amount to anything seeped into my psyche. I believed I was washed-up, used, good for nothing and that my "baggage" would make me undesirable. *"Nobody's going to want you." "Who's going to love you like I do?"* That sentence made me shiver. If this is love, I don't want it.

It's time I love me. I LOVE ME. When was that going to sink in? Who cares if nobody wanted me? The kids need me. I need me. I lived every day for two years feeling like I was worthless, like nothing I did mattered, like nothing I had was of value. I took up space and met everyone else's needs. I wasn't my own person. I was a space.

Schmoozy apologies always followed his put-downs. *"You know how sorry I am. I always feel like I'm not good enough for you. I know I can't do that anymore. I'll do better. I promise. I can't lose you. I can't lose myself."* He would somehow be more bothered by the idea of me leaving him. *"Baby,"* he'd plead with me. He never called me baby unless he was apologizing for something. *"You can't hate me any more than I hate myself."* The worst part about the whole thing was that I didn't hate him. I didn't hate him at all. I loved him. As much as I didn't want to, as much as I wanted to hate him, I couldn't. And that made me hate myself. I loved him, but I needed to love myself more.

CHAPTER SIXTEEN

Escalation - *Age 26*

The biggest lie he ever told me was *"I love you. I will never hurt you and will never forsake you."* The first time he hit me was the most painful thing I'd ever gone through, not only because of the physical pain and the black eye that resulted, but because, yet again, the one person who was supposed to protect me, who was supposed to be my biggest supporter, had broken my heart. If my heart was the only thing that suffered, I may have recovered faster. The second time was no different. I think it hurt worse than the first time because I had felt certain it wouldn't happen again.

The door creaked open, the bottle clicked, and the verbal onslaught ensued. After several years of being convinced I couldn't do anything right, I finally found my voice and asked why he drank so much.

"Why is the first thing you need when you come home a drink instead of a kiss from your wife or a hug from the kids? WHY?"

He pushed me. Completely ready for an argument, I braced myself to stand my ground. His eyes went cold, and venom spewed from his mouth as he spoke.

"WHY?!?! Are you asking me why? Why isn't the house clean? Why isn't dinner ready? Why are you such a lazy prude?"

I never expected him to put his hands on me. I opened my mouth to say something, but the only sound that escaped my lips was a grunt when he shoved me. I stumbled. Trying to keep my balance, I flung my body forward, expecting to fall. As I reached out for the handle of the cabinet door, he slammed it shut; it bounced back, hitting me in the mouth as a result. This was the first fat lip I had in my life. Immediately, his demeanor changed, and his hand flew to his mouth. I'd never seen a mood change that quickly before. My eyes burned as I fought back the tears, not because the door hit me in the face, and not because he called me a "mouthy bitch," but because, in that instant, as I could feel the swelling of my lip, he laughed. He laughed like it was funny, like it was healing for him. The monster was born.

"I'm sorry. That was funny," that laugh, the guffaw that painlessly escaped his belly, haunted me for years. The pleasure he saw in my pain was baffling.

I told people I fell. I tripped over the rug that clothed the hardwood floor. The fringed end was curled up just enough to catch my toe, and I tripped. I fell into the russet coffee table we conveniently bought the weekend before; it hit me in the mouth. As detailed and elaborate as my story was, still nobody believed me. They pretended to, but I knew they didn't. When someone falls, you ask them if they're ok and move on. You don't ask them repeatedly what happened and how they fell if you believe them. Technically, he didn't physically hit me this time. It was an accident. The door slipped out of his hands. He didn't *mean* to hit me in the mouth; it just happened. I told myself I got what I deserved, anyway. If I would have just kept my mouth shut and not antagonized him, it wouldn't have happened. He would never in a million years do it again. He told me so. So why make it real? I kept up with the clumsy farce. I would purposely trip in front of people so it didn't seem so questionable when I showed up with another black eye or another fat lip or a bruise on my cheek or a mark on my arm. "I fell" became just something I said. "How are you?" "I fell." The looks, the whispers, the random check-ins all received the same answer "I fell." And that was that.

Making dinner, I held Liam, who was babbling and content in my arms. While fighting back tears and listening to Dan saying how unfit I was to be a mother, I rested my cheek on the top of Liam's head and breathed in his scent. The orange glow emitting from the kitchen window signaled the setting sun, the brief lapse in time between day and night; sober and drunk; Jekyll and Hyde. Tiny fingers touched my face and I lovingly gummed them with my lips, pretending to eat them, which made him laugh, the greatest sound in the world. All is right in this perfect moment. I nibble, he laughs. We repeat this little game for several minutes.

The smack came out of nowhere.

"HEY!" I shouted, turning to face the man I was married to. Not knowing what set him off, I watched the cold come over him and his eyes glaze over as I felt the sting on my cheek. My jaw dropped open, and the heat spread across my cheek. Tears welled up and as I turned away, the familiar

touch I had come to know turned to pain. I attempted to walk past him. Liam started crying.

"I have to feed him," I said through gritted teeth.

"Shut him up, would ya?" He slurred. It sounded more like *"shumup woulja?"*

"He's a baby," I said a little angrier than intended. He put his finger in the baby's mouth a little too hard. I jerked away, shielding my son's face with my hand. Dan pushed me down into a chair and held my head to the table, pinching my ear in his hand while the other ear was bent, squished onto the glass. I pressed Liam against my chest; if my hand hadn't been behind his head, he would be squashed between me and the table, too. Afraid I was suffocating Liam, I pulled away with all of my might, forcing Dan to let go. With his middle finger jabbing into my face, I felt utterly worthless. For no apparent reason, I was disregarded.

Feeding the baby that night, I was so thankful for the distraction. That little boy looking me in the eyes was my reason. The boy in the bed next to him, clinging to my arm as he slept, was the motivation. The girl sleeping in the room next door was my purpose.

I gingerly tiptoed across the house to go to bed. Hoping Dan had fallen asleep, I had assumed incorrectly when I heard the unmistakable snap of a beer can opening. I sighed louder than I meant to, and he noticed.

"What?" he whispered.

"I want to go to bed. I'm tired." I desperately tried to portray. I was exhausted. Fighting to keep my eyelids open, I yawned. As soon as my head hit the pillow, I was certain I

would deeply slumber. I could fall asleep standing up. He grabbed my arm and pulled me in for a hug. His shoulder fit my head perfectly, and I relaxed too much into him. Willing my eyes not to close, I sighed.

"Have a beer with me," he probed.

"I'm so tired, I just want to go to bed."

His face scrunched up and his brow furrowed. *"Why are you tired? It's not like you did anything all day."*

I felt the anger bubbling up from the pit of my stomach. *"How dare you?"* I articulated. Throwing my hands up in disgust, I tried to scoot by him unscathed. He grabbed my hand and pulled me towards him. *"Please don't."* I pleaded. *"I just want to go to bed,"* I said as I yanked my hand from his.

"Dance with me." He grabbed my waist from behind and started swaying. Instead of fighting him, I conceded. If I denied him, he would just try harder the next night. If I gave in, he would leave me alone for at least a few days, so more often than not, I reluctantly acquiesced to appease him. I swung my hips a few times to placate him. He spun me around and kissed me on the nose. I flinched but forced a smile. I held my head up with great effort due to my pure exhaustion, but I didn't dare go to the bedroom. It would create an unwelcome invitation, so I compelled myself towards the living room. Deliriously exhausted, I plummeted my body onto the couch. Within seconds, I felt the cushion envelope my frame as I sank into it. Surrendering to the plush coziness of the velvety hug, I immediately fell asleep. What felt like mere minutes later, the discernible snap and hiss of a beer can opening woke me. In that groggy state, I could hear but not fully comprehend

what was going on. Fighting against my will, I robotically forced myself to bed. As soon as I pulled the blanket up to my chin, ready to shut out the world, a hungry wail came through the baby monitor. I couldn't stop the tears from falling. As I drug myself across the house, he murmured behind me:

"I'd feed him if I could, but I don't have milk jugs."

There were bottles of pumped milk in the fridge that would have taken 15 seconds to heat in the microwave, but I didn't have the energy to correct him.

As tired as I was, I could not let myself fall asleep while nursing. Fearing I would suffocate him in some way, I provided the life-giving liquid gold to my baby boy who didn't yet know the magnitude of blessing he brought to me. By the time he finished eating, my abuser was fast asleep, which saved me many hours of agony. I never welcomed a few hours of sleep more than I had in that moment.

Since I still had not satisfied my husband, I knew he would be even more ravenous tomorrow night. I would have to forget my exhaustion. My feelings didn't matter, my emotions weren't important, and my mood wasn't considered. Saying "I'm tired" or "I don't want to" had no bearing on what he wanted. When he wasn't drunk, he was affectionate and romantic, but I had forgotten what that was like. Dreading the next evening, I lied down. Sleep was worth it.

CHAPTER SEVENTEEN

Phoenix Rising - *Age 27*

The morning after each injury was skimmed over. He claimed he didn't do it because he "would never do that." He didn't do that because he "didn't remember doing it."

"If I don't remember, it didn't happen." "How can you apologize for something you don't remember?"

"I don't know... ask my father," I wanted to say.

There was no way it happened like that. I'm a liar. I'm a storyteller. I'm attention-seeking. I'm just clumsy. These were the lies he made me believe. I shrugged. I have never felt less like a person in my life than in those moments. He had a nickname for me which I completely hated. He knew it and used it anyway.

"It's cute," he'd say. *"Nobody else calls you that."* True, because I hate it. And he'd kiss me on the forehead. It took everything in me to not shudder. I don't like being kissed

on the forehead, especially if I'm being called a name that I hate. He held my hand in the kitchen as I tried to load the dishwasher.

"I love you," he murmured.

I nodded. *"Me too."* I wasn't lying in the slightest. This was what I knew of love. Love is pain. Love is scary. Love is surrendering your entire soul to another person and hoping they've got you. That's what my love was: a surrender. 'For better or worse' kept cycling in my brain. This was the 'worse.' It would have to get better. I would see him through this. The man I met was not this man. I would find him again. People make mistakes. People change. If nobody ever got a second chance, then nobody would ever be truly happy. It would be okay. He would be okay. We would be okay. All the thoughts I tried to make into reality. A deep sigh escaped my lips, and an accepting calm infiltrated my mind. He wouldn't do it again. It was a stupid night we didn't ever have to talk about again. I squeezed his hand. I would fix him. That's what I do. As I surrendered yet again, the click was loud enough to drown out my gasp. He carried around a plastic bottle in his pocket which I never knew was there.

The next time he hit me, we were arguing about the drinking again.

"Why is it so important?"

"To tolerate you," he said.

Maybe I was that bad. Maybe I was not meant to be anyone's wife. I was no good at it. I was good at being a mother. I knew that I was meant to do that. If you can't look your child directly in the eyes and believe they are the best thing that has ever happened to you, then you don't know.

They were always the reason I kept going. My face contorted in response to his statement.

"What exactly are you tolerating?"

"A wife who won't give it up, a wife who can't cook or clean, and a wife who is boring."

I wish having my character attacked didn't affect me, but he repeatedly mashed that button, and I snapped back.

"If you weren't drinking every second you're awake, I might be more attracted to you."

As I tried to slink past him to continue my nightly routine, which was all about getting the kids fed, bathed, and to sleep, he grabbed my arm.

"Let me go." I demanded.

He squeezed my arm a little too tight, so I dug my fingers around his hand, peeling it away from my arm. He forcibly shoved me away. I hit the coffee table and a picture frame fell to the floor.

Glass shattered. I heard the crunch and tinkle of the glass breaking before I heard the bang. Sharp fragments sprinkled across the living room floor. Seething with resentment, I fought back the tears. Picking up the picture still attached to the frame, it took every fiber of strength not to tear it up. I was smiling in the photo. I had no idea who that girl was. She was me, but I didn't recognize her. She was happy. He was standing behind me, arm across the front of my chest, squeezing my shoulder, and his chin was resting on the top of my head. My hand clutched his elbow while our other hands were interlocked. My smile is haunting. It's genuine. A wide, open-mouthed, gleaming-teeth, crinkled-eyes, full-faced smile. I couldn't stop the tears from falling. Where did she go?

The glass from the frame had exploded and scattered across the entire floor; the hardwood, the carpet, and the tile. Barefoot, I cautiously shuffled to the pantry to get the broom. I felt the sting of an invisible piece of glass entering my toe. Pulling it out with a groan, I started sweeping.

"I'll replace it," I whispered to myself.

"WHAT?!" he hissed.

"I was talking to myself. I said…"

Abruptly interrupting me and not allowing me to finish my thought, per usual, he started name-calling. *"I SAID I'LL REPLACE IT. The frame, not the picture. Just go to bed or keep drinking. I don't care."*

He knew he would get a response by attacking my character. When he called me a worthless nobody, I felt the exasperation stirring in my belly. I pushed him. He snatched the dustpan out of my hand and beat me over the head with it. Although it was flimsy and not very sturdy, anything that breaks while being used as a weapon is torturous. I crawled across the floor to get away from him, embedding glass shards into my hand in the process. Yanked by my hair across the floor with a foot to the face holding me down like the "piece of dirt" he said I was, I used the broom like a bat and started swinging. This was the first time I fought back. The puncture in my thumb left streaks of red everywhere I touched. Once he passed out, I was finally able to clean up the floor and my hand. Another night in a row, I cried myself to sleep reluctantly next to him.

The next morning, as loving, fatherly and husbandly as he could be, he handed me breakfast in bed and played with the kids in the yard like nothing ever happened. With an "I'm sorry baby" and a kiss on the forehead, an "it won't happen again" or "don't do that again" remark, it was forgotten by him. Maybe if I hadn't provoked him, he wouldn't have acted that way. Maybe if I just let him have his way with me, he wouldn't get upset and we could have uneventful nights. Maybe if I just did what he wanted, it wouldn't be like this. Leaving was not as easy as just picking up and going. The alarm bells were sounding in my head to figure it out, but the angst in my heart made me believe I was the problem. If I changed my attitude, he would change his. This is MY fault. I made him this way. I could change him back.

The night he put his hands around my neck, I thought it was too late. I was in too deep, and my toleration of his criticism had gotten us to this point. With my gradual acceptance of his disrespect, I permitted this behavior and normalized it. I saw the change in his eyes. They went dark and cold. This was a look I knew all too well. It was becoming far too common, the tunnel vision.

I heard them before I saw them. The kids screamed, *"Stop daddy!"* And *"Mommy!"* I looked up and the children were standing in the hallway. I wanted to tell them to go to their rooms, to look away. The only thing going through my mind was that tonight was the night I was going to die and they were going to see it. Wide-eyed Noah was clinging to his sister, tears streaming down his face. I closed my eyes and mouthed, "I'm sorry." As I turned my face to look at Dan, my hands clawing at his, I saw the change in his eyes. They warmed up, his face softened and he just… let go. My lungs burned as I gasped for air. I scurried across the floor to the kids and shoved them into Liam's room. Locking the door behind me, I wept, clinging to each of them. Dan was sobbing on the other side of the door. *"I'm sorry, I'm sorry. I'm sorry."* He was pleading.

I had no money, no access to the money, and nowhere to go. He had hid my cell phone and the car keys. The phone had been ripped out of the wall the day prior, so I had no way to contact anyone. I knew once he passed out, he wasn't waking up for a while. And, once he did, he would be sober and non-violent, so my only option was to wait until morning. He was rational and logical when he wasn't drinking, so my choice was to wait and talk to him. Somehow, I didn't think he could forget this incident like he so easily seemed to do. How do you black out every single night and do unthinkable things and not remember any of them? He never ceased to amaze me, and never in a good way.

I woke up with all three children draped around me. I laid there for a long while, just holding onto my babies for dear life. They were my lifeline. What questions would they have? How traumatized would they be? What would I tell them? How do I protect them if I can't even protect myself? Right on cue, the baby wakes up for a feeding. My breast was bruised and hurt so badly that I couldn't let him latch on. I don't even know how or when that happened. Thankfully, I had started supplementing with formula the week before. Reluctantly, I walked out of the room. After one step, I stopped and listened. I took another few steps on my tiptoes, barely making a sound. I could hear the squish of the carpet beneath my feet. I was still wearing my jeans from yesterday. A bottle was made and sitting on the counter, on top of a sliver of paper with five simple words. I'M SORRY. PLEASE FORGIVE ME. I noticed my reflection in the microwave glass. I could see the fingerprints on my throat and the bruising already appearing. There's no way that would be explained away by a fall.

His narcissistic, self-absorbed ways somehow convinced me that it was my fault. He seemed to know what I was thinking. One night, as I was contemplating my life and my options, he looked at me and told me that I'll never be able to leave him because he will always find me. I swore he had found the bag I had packed in my bottom drawer. He truly made me believe that I either made it up or I did it to myself. I thought I was crazy.

He believed something strong enough that he eventually thought it was the truth, and he sold it hard enough that I began to question what I thought was the truth. I gave everything I had, and he took it all. Everything was my fault. Everything I did caused him to react that way. He apologized profusely. I begged him to get help, to quit drinking. He was loving and caring and adoring when he wasn't drinking. He promised he would, and I also demanded that I have access to money and the car at all times. What if there was an emergency with the kids? He agreed. I gave him an ultimatum: me or the drinking. I held the baby all day, not once putting him down. I was terrified he was injured or distressed by the night's events. I left with the kids for a night. We went to a hotel and I paid cash so he couldn't look at the bank account and see where I was. He called my cell phone 47 times that night. I should have stayed gone, but with his fear that I actually might, he promised yet again that he would quit drinking.

He didn't pick up a drink for two whole weeks. Maybe it was working. Anyone can do anything if they really want to.

During that time, he was kind, caring, and devoted. He went to outpatient rehab and AA meetings every night for 14 days. He came straight home afterwards and appreciated what I had on the table for dinner, even when it was another night of mac and cheese. He was respectful and understood no meant no. But, in all honesty, his willingness to help with the kids and express gratitude made him more attractive to me. Finally, I had won against something. Finally, I was worth more than something. I wasn't gasping for air anymore. I could exhale deeply. He chose me.

CHAPTER EIGHTEEN

High Hopes - *Age 27*

It was short-lived. I'd hoped he could overcome this just like my father had. I knew alcoholism is a trait that could be passed down to your children, and their children, and so on. I wasn't on that track, but in my mind, maybe I was drawn to him because he reminded me of my father. I had lost so many years with my father, but when he finally got back on the wagon and rode it for a very long time, our relationship had grown exponentially. I became "daddy's little girl" at 21 years old, but it didn't matter. I had hope for the same outcome for my marriage. My husband would eventually realize his family was more important than the bottle. If my father could do it, he surely could. I had hope, I had faith, and I had love. The trifecta. It could work.

He was doing better, I thought. Or maybe I just put my blinders back on because I didn't want to believe I was the second choice yet again. I was always the second choice. I was never good enough to be the first choice. I couldn't keep a man. I believed I drove them to drink and caused their destructive behavior. I was the problem. It was all I could think about. What did I do? What could I do? Why was this happening? I truly believed he was getting better. He'd come straight home after work, exhausted. I didn't question it. He worked hard all day. What I didn't know was that he either hid a bottle under the mattress, and he would claim exhaustion and drink himself into a stupor, then wake up a few hours later, completely well-rested and high-functioning so I didn't pay attention, or he would drink all day and come home to sleep. Changing the sheets one day, I found the bottle stashed under the mattress. It took everything in me not to dump it and confront him or leave it out in plain sight so he knew that I knew, but I decided to put it back and watch more closely. I would be more aware. Was I that oblivious? Did I really have that many false hopes? Maybe I was as stupid as he kept saying I was. How did I miss this?

CHAPTER NINETEEN

The Sunflower - *Age 16*

My dad had once said, good or bad, you will never forget your first love. The first relationship I'd ever been in set the bar high, but the heartbreak that came from it was nearly enough to guard my heart forever. I never wanted to feel that kind of pain again in my lifetime. The pain that came from that breakup was almost too much to bear. When you give your heart to another person completely and wholly, with every fiber of your being, it feels impossible to get it back. He looked at me with admiration, respect and awe. I was on a pedestal I didn't deserve to be on for absolutely no reason at all, and I was certain every day that I would fall off. It was way too high up there. I was just a girl. With so much damage already done, the wound barely held together with the thread of self-dignity I had remaining, I couldn't justify my worth. I was dumbfounded by what he saw in me; this quiet, restrained, guarded girl with a longing to simply be seen. He made me feel normal. He made me feel. The day it ended and I had to give up my safety net, I hurt like I had never hurt before. This wasn't intentional like so many before. We were torn apart for reasons out of our control, and even though it was necessary, it felt wrong. I jumped off that pedestal and ran straight for despair. I would have done anything to numb the pain. It was a soul-crushing pain I never fully recovered from. Everything happens for a reason, I told myself. What was the reason for this? Why was everything good taken from me? I still haven't answered that question.

I was a fragile doll made of glass. One wrong move and I would shatter into a million pieces. He holds the missing piece that would put me back together. He looked at me and time stood still. The clock froze. The number 143 was still on the pager. Our secret language that meant "I love you". His smile burned in my mind. He saw me. He didn't just notice me — he SAW me. He saw into the depths of my soul. The place in which he now lives with that little piece of my heart he will always have.

I'm a delicate sunflower. My bruised and battered existence longs for delicacy, the touch that only I know. The touch meant only for me. I could hear his voice in my ear telling me I'm beautiful, and I started to believe it. The way his eyes danced across my body made me feel safe in his presence. Now, I just feel as if I've gone astray. I'm broken. The stagnant minutia of my depreciating self-worth resounds in my mind. What he saw in me, I'll never know, but he shaped my entire being. He'll never know the extent of it, but I am who I am because of him. I felt so alive, just being near him. I saw him from across the room before he saw me. Time slowed down. I was moving in slow motion, gliding across the floor, my hair swaying with every step. I couldn't get to him fast enough. The crowd silenced. I could see their lips moving, but no sound was reaching my ears. I kept walking with intent.

Nothing mattered except placing my hand into his like a glove. He smiled. My heart skipped a beat. I longed for that heartbeat, to feel the warmth of his lips on mine. I smiled through the pain. I painted a picturesque, idyllic mask and faced the day. My satiety was incomplete and I was a shallow rendition of who I made myself out to be. There's no one like him, and I haven't been the same since. He made me feel whole. He knew me in a way nobody else ever will. The library of intimacy is deadlocked, and only I hold the key. The void is deep. The hole will forever be unfilled, covered up with creases held together by glue, but never completely devoid of space. I reach out my hand and grab nothing. I need water, firm soil, and the sun to thrive, but my sun is burning out.

Just as the sunflower follows the sun, I would surely follow him, for I needed him to continue to grow. My limbs are weak, but even in the darkness, the sunflower continues to flourish. I shrink with the changing of the seasons, my petals dry out and fall off, but my roots remain embedded in the soil. With the right amount of sunlight, I will bloom again.

He planted the seed, I reaped the embodiment of his nurturing, and although I will forever long for the sun, I must know how to climb to the moon. I have to face my own reflection. The foundation of my stalk is firm, and I inch closer to the freedom of the night. I know if I fall, there is no one there to catch me.

The dimple in his chin, the way he tilts his head back when he laughs, and the skip in his step when he sees me (although he thinks I don't notice) is what I will take with me. The deep impact he left on my titanic Armageddon is what I will base my entire relational life on, and he may never know it. I'll look over my shoulder for the last time with the mixed *tape of emotions on my sleeve and forever look to the sun for direction and purpose while basking in the glory of it on top of my own mountain.*

The sun is bright today, and I'm a little bit better.

As a low-maintenance flower, the sunflower can withstand any weather. I find it pretty and sturdy. Although not as beautiful as a rose, it is also not as delicate. The sunflower is my favorite flower today.

CHAPTER TWENTY

The Worst Night - *Age 28*

Statistics show that an abused woman will leave — or attempt to leave — an average of seven times before finally leaving for good. I can attest to that. I kept going back. The number one question I was always asked was, *"Why didn't you leave? Why did you stay?"* I felt this was the equivalent of asking a rape victim, "Why did you wear that? Why didn't you say no?" Instead of asking, "Why did he do that?"

Why was I the problem? I was already questioning myself daily. "What did I do? I must have done something to cause this. I need to change my attitude, my posture, or my body language. I need to change how I behave. I need to change who I am." I thought I could fix him. I thought love was enough. I believed I did something to cause this, so if I stopped provoking him, he would stop reacting. The kids deserved to be raised by two parents. With no job and no money, I had nowhere to go. I felt stuck. All my friends had slowly gone away, and I didn't want to disappoint my family, his family, and myself.

Before he fell ill, my father moved to be near to me. Then I became his caretaker, and I couldn't leave him behind. I've always put myself at the bottom of the totem pole, so this wasn't any different. Dan apologized and promised he wouldn't do it again. Continuously disappointed as a child, I always kept my promises, so I relied on that. It was a gradual progression; it wasn't as if he just hit me for no reason one day. I had tolerated so much up to that point; I felt as if I were less and less of a person each day until verbal and emotional abuse turned physical.

I remember an acquaintance telling me she envied my relationship. *"He adores you… I want that."* I was so good at pretending we were the perfect couple that even I believed it. I only put on social media what I wanted to show. Nobody knows what goes on behind closed doors except for the two people behind them. And I wouldn't open that door to show anyone unless I was ready to invite them in. It's something to always remember — unless you are in that house and are living each moment they are, you shouldn't be covetous. It's one of the ten commandments for a reason. I only showed what I wanted to. Most people do. I hid the abuse for years because I was ashamed, scared, and belittled. In my mind, nobody would care. I wanted so much to be accepted, loved, and acknowledged that I ignored my own suffering in order to be seen. I believed nobody would want me; that nobody wanted a woman with kids. "Nobody would want you now," he'd remind me. Then the threats would come: he has the house, the job, and the money, so he would get the kids, and I would never see them again. I truly believed it.

The main reason I stayed? I loved him. I strongly felt that love really did conquer all and that loving him was enough. Does that answer the question? All of those things I thought were wrong.

Nothing lasts forever. Everyone has a breaking point. There were no police reports up to this point. How would I ever be taken seriously, that this was a regular and consistent thing, if I'd never reported it before? Most first-time offenders get a slap on the wrist, which leads to further feelings of inadequacy and abuse. He would look like a first-timer and get away with it until it happened again, and I would have to report it again. I wasn't sure it was worth it. I told myself I had to change my demeanor and stop being provocative. My childhood abuser blamed me. My mother blamed me. He blamed me. Maybe I *was* the problem.

I had left the relationship — either physically or emotionally — three times already. People often asked, *"Why did you keep going back?"* It's a question I wish I could answer. Maybe I am a glutton for punishment. Maybe he had this spell on me I couldn't break. Maybe he was a bad guy, but I wanted to be loved so badly that I ignored it.

The silver-tongued deceiver and his superfluous pleas were convincing. His histrionic performance and adamant denial insulted my intelligence. When he insinuated my lucidity was lacking, I began to question my sanity. With the fairytales he concocted, I began to doubt my reality. Though I suspected manipulation, he led me to believe the accounts of it were figments of my imagination. His insidious deceit left me frantically examining my equanimity. Was I rational? Was he?

He told a beautiful engagement story, how he got down on one knee, when in actuality, we got married on a whim at the courthouse. Was I wrong? He loquaciously told the romantic story so many times that I even started including details I saw in my head that... never happened. And my recollection of things that DID happen, he insisted I made up. I struggled with my truth and his lies. Thus began the gaslighting; he lit the match and fueled the fire.

Everything was exaggerated. I started to wonder what was real and what was all in my head. Confused, I was easily brain-washed into thinking I was the problem. Could it get any worse? I didn't realize how much I didn't want the answer to that question.

It's hard to admit this, but we had the most fun together when we were both drinking. Was it because I cared less? Or I simply understood him more, I don't know. He'd conveniently forget the good times though, too. He claimed I was boring and mundane on any average day.

"Have a drink. Loosen up a bit," he'd tease.

If I didn't, I was a prude. And if I did, I indulged too much. Hey kettle? You're black. But of course, only *my* actions were under scrutiny. I noticed I had to keep refilling my wine glass, yet I hadn't taken many sips. If I said anything, I was blaming him. Yet, if I didn't, I was judged and criticized for drinking too much.

"You already went through one bottle." He winked.

The tongue is the heaviest thing to hold. I bit it so hard, I choked on the blood. However, on vacation, sans kids, or special occasions, I matched him drink for drink. We laughed, danced, and forgot. Things were okay for a bit. We enjoyed each other's company and eventually I recognized that drinking made it easy. I could make a bottle of liquor last for months. One Friday evening, I poured a mixed drink and immediately recognized it tasted diluted. Dumping it out and trying again with no change, I poured straight from the bottle. Water. I could only assume he polished off my citrus vodka and replaced it with water. Irritated, I tossed the whole bottle and poured myself a glass of wine instead.

In all the violent nights which resulted in injuries, that was the night enough was finally enough. I had a small window of opportunity, and I crawled out of it. The police were called only one other time, but when they had showed up, I had sent them away. Because there were no visible marks and I insisted that all was okay, they left. The report stated, "suspected domestic violence, but no proof and non-cooperative occupants result in no action. Watch for repeat." As I read it, I winced. Secrets aren't secrets for long. Eventually, the truth reveals itself.

The night was eerily gloomy with wind whipping off the house, howling through the trees. The moon hid behind stormy clouds which were sporadically illuminated by streaks of lightning that lit up our dark living room as well, and distant claps of periodic thunder, all presenting a good old-fashioned southern thunderstorm.

Immersed in a book, I forgot I was at the mercy of my captor. As he settled in to watch a movie, a quick glance my way directed his attention to the wine glass resting on the table next to me. The second living room which we had turned into my home office was where I usually enjoyed my down time. I felt most comfortable in the jumbo recliner I often slept in before the 40" wall-mounted television where I watched my "programs." The lightbulb in the lamp on my desk had burned out, and I hadn't gotten around to replacing it. It needed a spiral light bulb with low wattage, but it emitted a perfectly relaxing amount of light. The base of the lamp flashed bubbles that spun around, imitating a lava lamp. The swirls and colors that reflected off the wall soothed me. Making a mental note to get that bulb, I cozied up on the couch in the family room, the main living room where the 75" big screen TV — his pride and joy — sat, often untouched. The red leather cowhide couch perched against the wall atop the oak floor looked pristine, as it was rarely sat on. With one leg tucked underneath me and my elbow resting on the arm of the sofa, I pulled my pink plush blanket up to my waist and lost myself in someone else's story. He pushed the cuddler — the giant two-seater recliner that I used as a bed when it was the only place I could get comfortable enough to sleep during my last pregnancy — into the family room directly in front of me. He engrossed himself in a loud, action-packed, raunchy movie, and I couldn't have seen the screen if I wanted to. At a quiet point in the movie, I heard the distinct rustle of the brown paper bag he discreetly shoved into the pocket of the cushion, then the click of the cap I struggled to ignore. The explosion of the television startled me and I gasped, dropping my book. *"SHHH!"* he hissed at me. Rolling my eyes and boring into the back of his head, I willed him to pass out. When he was drinking, I couldn't breathe easily or read a book without upsetting him. I couldn't concentrate on the words of my book because of the intensity and the volume of the movie.

"Can you turn it down?" I timidly mumbled.

His lazy stuttered response, *"Noooo. I'm watching a movie,"* bothered me more than it should have. I briefly considered going to my room to read, but lying in bed would be considered an invitation, and there was definitely no party I wanted to attend.

"Come sit with me." I could hardly hear over the commotion.

"Hmm?"

He asked again a bit louder. *"COME SIT. Watch the movie and hold my hand and stuff."*

"I'm fine. Watch your movie, but can you please turn it down? The kids are sleeping."

"The kids are fine."

"They won't be if they get woken up. Does it really have to be that loud?"

"Why do you complain about everything I do? Just read your stupid book and drink your drinky drink and let me watch my movie." He said it with a few choice words mixed in.

The simplest of requests always resulted in an argument. If I just kept quiet, there would be no more issues. He would finish his bottle and go to sleep, and all would be well. I told myself not to say another word.

My father had died only days prior. I had just picked up his ashes that afternoon. Rubbing the side of the box he rested in, I felt a sense of relief wash over me. I couldn't afford a fancier urn, and I felt unsatisfied; he deserved better. Reaching for the baby monitor, I set it on the end table next to the box and turned it up to max volume. I heard the baby's sigh come through and relaxed a little. I wasn't in the mood for a fight, or a cuddle. Or anything really. I just wanted to be left alone. I sunk further down into the couch, rested my head on the back pillow and opened my book again to try and drown out the noise... and my grief.

At the next quiet point in the movie, I turned the page of my book. It caught the edge of my blanket and made a sound like ripping paper. I winced.

"Can I just watch a movie?" He screeched at me. I stuttered, completely blindsided when the book was ripped from my hands and tossed across the room.

"HEY!" I protested. As I started to stand, he pushed me back down on the couch.

"Please stop." I pleaded with him.

"Why are you such a prude?" he spat. A member of his family had recently died too, so I wanted to give him the benefit of the doubt. But to be honest, I was tired of making excuses for him. There was always a reason for his outbursts.

"Just go to bed. Keep drinking and just pass out. Please."

He always reacted when I defended myself. Before I could say another word, the end table next to me flew. My father's ashes, along with my glass half-full of wine, hit the ground. At the time, I couldn't afford anything other than a plain white cardboard box with a laminated sticker plastered on the side that revealed his name, date of death, and other seemingly unimportant letters that identified him for his final resting place. Already mortified enough that he had been placed in something I brought cereal home in, seeing his ashes fly through the air was the most demoralizing thing I had ever experienced. It was as if I was watching it in slow motion. With my filter gone at this point, I stammered through clenched teeth and streaming tears.

"The only thing I find solace in is that he died never knowing you were a monster." I attempted to scamper past him to pick the box up off the floor when I felt his hand on the back of my head. *"Please stop."* I whispered.

Hot tears flowed freely down my cheeks, and I didn't care. The burning of my scalp where he had yanked my hair nearly from its roots, and the disrespect towards my father, left me in heaps on the floor. The box was lying face down and his insolence toward my father was incomprehensible. Reaching the box and cradling it in my hands, I sobbed. Not for me or my situation, but for my father. I couldn't even mourn him properly. The fire flew from my eyes as I stared at Dan, willing him to pass out. To drink himself to such a stupor I could clean up, and mourn, and read, and do whatever else I wanted to do fearlessly. I heard the soft close of the door leading out to the garage where his not-so-secret stash was hidden. Most nights, it bothered me that he went out there to get his fix. But, that night, I was thankful for it. For a split second, I considered locking the door and keeping him out there. I was beyond devastated that my father was so blatantly disregarded without a morsel of regret, but I always tried to be the bigger person, always tried to do the better thing. I always gave him the benefit of the doubt. This time, I knew there weren't enough apologies in the world. Silently, but with vengeance in my blood, I stewed. Too angry to sleep, too upset to calm down, and too sad to concentrate on reading again, with eyes red and puffy from crying, I logged into my computer. I had work reports to complete which I knew would occupy my mind enough to settle me. I had started a job as a medical transcriptionist recently. It was something I could do from home during my down time to contribute to the household expenses. I stiffened when he walked back in. His silhouette entered the doorway. An apology was an ear length away. My computer pinged and I cowered.

*"Who's tha*t?" The words spit from his mouth. *"WHOS THAT?!"* When I didn't answer.

"No one." I knew what was coming before it happened. The glass L-shaped table that housed my computer flipped upside-down in one movement. The glass splintered and my computer cracked. He backed me into the wall, and the room quieted as he repeatedly slapped me in the ear.

It all started because I had turned the page of my book too loudly.

"Cheater" echoed in my head as my ears rang relentlessly.

Convinced I was cheating with all of them, I wasn't allowed to converse with male friends. The saying "Happy Wife, Happy Life" is valid. A woman who is loved completely and wholly protects and nurtures the relationship. When I was completely invested in the relationship, I cherished him. But when I was disregarded, unacknowledged, and disrespected, I let a door open that allowed others in where they shouldn't be. I permitted certain comments and ignored prior boundaries. Perhaps I was seeking the attention I craved; the loving kind and not the hurtful one. I feared Dan. I shut out anyone who might have been perceived as a threat to avoid the name-calling and verbal thrashing I despised. I was devoted to Dan, but my fear of him controlled me. I had talked to one particular friend pretty regularly since high school. It was never more than a friendship; a confidante of sorts. I never brought up anything about my relationship or the troubles within it, but we frequently talked about his. I seemed to have it all together, so my advice was sought after on how to handle domestic situations. I was not an expert, but I was excellent at giving advice; though I never took my own. Not that it mattered. I could have been talking to Dan's grandmother and the result would have been the same. This was a minor incident compared to previous nights, but it was the last straw. This was the night I had wanted to come for so long, but I didn't realize it until that moment. There went my job, my only saving grace, in fragments of broken glass.

This was the night he finally got arrested. *"I'm done,"* I said in barely a breath. Certain he would come at me again, since there was nothing else to break, I planted my foot and stood my ground. A little louder, I sighed, *"I'm done. We're getting a divorce and you can wallow in your self-pity but I won't be your punching bag anymore."*

"I never hit you, you psycho c—. Go f— yourself. I'll be in the garage waiting for the cops," he promised.

Unlike the many times before, and with my small window of opportunity, I finally called 911.

I had come to this point several times before, but I never got this far. The phone was either snatched from my hand with crocodile tears and groveling or I just wasn't strong enough to follow through. I didn't pursue it. Shock, anger, fear... one of those emotions took over.

When the officers showed up, I had a fleeting thought of sending them away again. The same female officer I sent away the last time returned. She had left her card with a note that said "Call us if you need us," but I had thrown it away the second they left. Even they knew. But without a corroborating witness or a victim, no crime had taken place. Little did they know, my long sleeves hid bruises and bloody scratches I never showed them. Why didn't they ask me to take my sunglasses off while I was inside my house? Ignorance is bliss. For them and for me, I suppose. Unbeknownst to me, verbal abuse and emotional abuse was still domestic violence. I didn't think I had a leg to stand on. The two officers spoke to each other at the front door for a moment, the red and blue lights flashing off the stark white of our house. Neighbors would certainly be out to see what was taking place. It took everything in me to continue talking to the officer.

"I'll talk to the victim," I overheard her tell her partner. Victim. That word struck a nerve. I had never taken on the role of a victim. Despite all the terrible things that had happened to me in my life that far, I never saw myself as a victim.

"Where is… is he your husband?" she asked me.

All I could do was nod. The male officer walked into my living room, asking for a description. A barefoot man with cargo shorts and a white t-shirt had been walking down the street when they pulled in the driveway.

"That's him," I nodded.

"I'll go talk to him," and he walked down the street after him.

Giving my statement with my infant son in my arms, now wide-awake in the middle of the night, I rocked back and forth. It's all I could muster. She sympathetically put her hand on my shoulder.

"Want to tell me what happened?" she asked me.

"I don't even know. He drinks and just gets mean. I don't even know what I did this time."

"Why is your ear red? Did he hit you?" All I could do was nod and sob silently. I wasn't sure what hurt worse... the fact that it got to this point, or the throbbing of my ear. *"Do you want to press charges? It might not be up to you, but it's important to know where your head's at,"* she stated thoughtfully.

"I don't want him to be arrested, at least not in front of the kids. I just want him to leave for the night so I can breathe." I tried to say through broken sniffles.

"If it's a DV call, someone goes to jail. But at the very least, we can remove him from the property for the night to cool down. Any other damage?" I pointed at the office. She meandered over to the broken glass, upturned table, and scattered papers. *"Did he do this?"* She compassionately questioned.

"I tossed the papers and flipped the chair because I didn't think you'd come if there wasn't enough damage." I wept a bucket of tears.

"Oh honey. How long has this been going on?" I started to answer when the male officer walked Dan in through the front door. The male officer asked matter-of-factly if I told him I wanted a divorce. Afraid of the aftermath, I froze. I couldn't speak.

"Do you want him to leave the premises?" he blurted out. *"Ma'am?"* I'd never felt more pressured. With glossy, blood-shot eyes, the drunken, belligerent man who had vowed

to protect me stared at me with a look I hadn't seen before. How would he react if the police left after I had called them? I suddenly found my voice.

"Yes." I said as clearly as I could. His cantankerous ego took over and he showed his true colors.

"This is my house. You leave." He pointed at me. *"Better yet —"* as he turned to face the officer *"— YOU leave."*

Putting his hand on Dan's arm, the male officer pleaded with him. *"Don't make me cuff you in front of the kids. Let's go outside and talk."*

"Don't touch me. I didn't hit her. I never hit her," he asserted.

The female officer chimed in with, *"Why is her ear red?"*

"She hit me first!" He accused, using his usual defense.

"And her property?" They both inquired.

"That's my property. I let her use it and she talks to other men."

I vehemently shook my head, and the hand on my shoulder eased my anxiety. I started to say something, and she interrupted with questions about why he destroyed his own property.

Noticing his bloody toe, the male officer asked him, *"What happened there?"*

My guess was he had either cut it on glass from the table or injured it when he went walking barefoot. Certain he would say I caused it, I clung to my baby even tighter. When the male officer requested that he go outside to talk some more and tell his version of the story, Dan refused.

"I'm going to ask you one more time…" before Dan could finish that statement, he was swung around and cuffed. At his own doing, he was charged with domestic violence. Yet, somehow, it was still my fault in his mind.

In a state of shock, feeling completely numb, I asked if I could tend to the kids. They were all awake and crying. All I wanted to do was leave.

"You can pick up a police report tomorrow morning. Is there anywhere you can go?" She asked me.

"Will he come back here?" I mumbled.

"Him? He's going to jail tonight. He won't see a judge until Friday, so you have 24 hours at least." It was Veterans Day, which gave me an extra day.

"Am I able to leave? Can I just pack up and go?"

She rubbed my shoulder and told me calmly, *"I can't tell you what to do, but you do what you need to keep yourself and your kids safe."*

I never forgot that advice. I knew you weren't allowed to leave if there was a pending investigation, but the case would be up to the DA now. My job was done. It was the hardest, yet the easiest phone call I ever made. The first step is the hardest, but all you must do is take it. The only other quote that stuck with me is that no man is worth your tears, but once you find one that is, he won't make you cry. I hope that sticks with you, too.

CHAPTER TWENTY-ONE

I Fled - *Age 28*

I fled. After multiple failed attempts at calling the police, broken phones and shattered computers, I finally fled. I left my home and everything in it while he was away, with just my children, the clothes we were wearing, and a box or two of valuables, including my father's ashes, tucked safely in the seat next to me. Dan rarely left me alone for fear of me doing just this, but I had one chance and a small window in which to leave. I was 28 years old and suddenly a single mother of three, one of whom was only an infant. I was a battered, bruised, and broken-down shell of a person simply trying to survive. He had demolished every ounce of my being. My soul was crushed. I had spent every day of the previous two years waiting for the next smack across my face, punch to the head, or kick to the stomach. I spent two years thinking there was no way out and that my entire life would be controlled by this man. When I ate, when I slept, when I spoke, and when I could leave the house were all up to him, because he made me feel so small and criticized everything I did, made, and said. When

I did leave the house, he was so convinced of infidelity that how long I could be gone and who I could go with were chosen for me. In attempts to cover the bruises or red marks, he would pick out an outfit for me, selling how good I looked in it, which contradicted everything he said about me going out in the first place. With my spirit damaged and my self-worth brutalized, I had a small glimmer of hope, and I took it. With my kids in tow, I fled. He was right that I truly didn't have any place to go, but at that moment, it didn't matter. I was heavily sobbing as I pulled out of the driveway, his cruel words repeating in my head. *"Nobody will love you ever again. Nobody will want you. You will never make it without me. You are worthless, useless, hopeless. Nobody will treat you the way I did."* I sure hoped not. *Worthless, worthless, worthless.* It was all I could hear reverberating in my head. Every time I considered turning around, the word grew louder. Looking in the rear-view mirror and seeing the kids finally dozing off, I understood the feeling of your entire heart walking around outside your body. They felt safe enough to sleep. They knew I had them. What they had witnessed and experienced was more than they ever should have. *"I got you,"* I whispered to them. *"Mama's got you."* Pulling out of our neighborhood, I headed to the only place I knew with the remaining funds in my dad's bank account: home.

With no time to feel sorry for myself, I could hardly process what had happened over the previous few weeks. With the death of my father and the death of my marriage, I was broken. Unsure where to go from that point, I had never felt so lost. When you've hit rock bottom, the only way to go is up. I didn't put myself in that situation completely, but I was going to get out of it. How? I hadn't a clue, but I promised my three little people I would figure it out. I drove all day, making calls the whole way. Within a matter of days, I got an apartment and set up interviews for temporary jobs. Faith and caffeine are the only reasons this happened so fast.

He called me forty-seven times over the next few days. In one voicemail, *"I'm sorry. Please. Come home. Thank you for calling the police. It changed me. I will do whatever you want. Just please come home. I love you and the kids so much. Please, I'm sorry."* Not even 10 seconds later, the next one, *"You b—. I hate you. How could you do this to me? You stole my kids, you psycho. Bring my kids back here right now or you'll never see them again."* The reverse psychology he tried on me messed with my emotions. *"Nobody will believe you. You left in the middle of the night with the kids with no explanation. Everybody knows I was the perfect husband and father, so you'll be the bad guy. They'll all feel sorry for me, and all your friends will know how horrible you are. How could you do something like this? You're crazy."*

Maybe so. I didn't have to prove anything to anyone. I'd hoped he would tell them his irrational story, and those who believed him could have him. Whether they knew my side of his story was not my concern. Showing my babies what I would and would not tolerate — and that they came first no matter what — became my priority. It took years to undo damage he managed to cause in mere minutes.

He was so good at manipulation; he would convince anyone who listened to his foolishness that I was the bad guy. I was okay with that. They could breathe in his toxin and become infected by his poison if they chose to do so. I would not defend him anymore. Or at least I would try not to. That was easier said than done.

Moving into this shady little apartment was terrifying. Not only did I have to learn how to live on my own, but I had to learn to love myself again. I ultimately was damaged goods, but I wasn't going to merely repackage myself just so I could be put back on the shelf. I didn't want to be held together with tape. I needed to be rebranded. An entirely different product: a new version of myself that could not only survive but thrive. The only person I had to prove it to was myself. Reflecting on the worst night of my life and how desperately terrified I was to move into this subpar building, I'm reminded of where I started and how far I've come. That dubious complex, as questionable as it was, has a soft spot in my heart. When I didn't know which way was up, that cramped dwelling showed me my worth. It gave me my confidence, my hope, and my zest for life back.

I couldn't begin to heal until I was physically away from him. I was able to breathe, yet constantly looking over my shoulder. Forgetting I didn't need permission to go anywhere or do anything, I still felt completely out of my element. A temp job turned into a permanent one, and self-sufficiency soon followed.

CHAPTER TWENTY-TWO

Finding My Way - *Age 29*

I didn't even know what I wanted, but I knew this wasn't it. I had already felt unlovable and unworthy of anything good after a lifetime of heartache, grief, and anguish. Trying to navigate life as a single mother was tiresome. I didn't know what love was until I figured out what love wasn't.

There must be something better for me. I was meant for greatness, but something always held me back. I suffered through abandonment, loss, neglect, abuse, and mistreatment my entire life. There were only a handful of people that I could ever truly trust, and even they had left me. I had known heartbreak like no other. The corruption of everything good in me left me bitter and distraught,but I forged on. I had three little people that relied on me and needed me to be okay, so I covered up the pain, masked the hurt, hid the tears, and plowed through my internal storm. There was no day like the present. He couldn't hurt me anymore. He tried hourly to invade my mentality, but it wasn't him that got to me. It was my own afflictions.

There was nothing unfamiliar about him. He was warm and charming with a venom that poisoned my soul. His toxicity wrapped around me and I couldn't escape. Like a python constricting my freedom, he stripped me of all I knew. I was drawn to him in a way I couldn't explain. Little did I know, once he got his claws in, the scars would remain forever.

I was a helper, a nurturer by nature. I knew that about myself from an early age. I was inclined to save everyone in some way. Whether they needed a hug, a hand or a smile, I gave without a second thought. I offered it to everyone, for nobody got special treatment. Every single person I came into contact with was immediately entranced. According to some, I was scintillating. My aura seemed to be welcoming and inviting. There wasn't a soul who disliked me... except for one. It wasn't hatred or distaste; it was pure obsession. He was obsessed with ensuring nobody else could ever see me smile, laugh, or dance around the living room. He burned out my light with every verbal onslaught of poisonous attacks. He was weakening the walls that I spent years trying to cement. Slowly spiraling downwards, my buoyant effervescence was flattening. I felt suffocated and believed there was no way out.

I survived a motherless home. Without the female empowerment and the womanly guidance I longed for, I was self-taught. Thankfully, I had women in my life that gave a damn and taught me how to be a woman, but I knew in the deepest places of my heart that they weren't my mother. I felt betrayed, abandoned, and left by her, the one person who was meant to protect me. She did for so long, but she didn't choose me in the end. I was never the first choice. That's when the unloved, unwanted, unworthy feelings began. So when this deviant convinced me he was good for me, I ignored the warning signs and fell into his trap, a trap it took me a long time to free myself from. In some ways, I still was not free, even after I escaped physically. I deeply desired to feel safe, to feel truly wanted for who I was and not what I could offer. I was alone with a child and already felt I didn't belong or didn't deserve the world even though it was at my fingertips. I was treading water to try and remain afloat, but my ship was sinking.

I had a good intuition. I trusted myself, except when I was with him. He made me believe I was the problem and he had promised to "fix" me. I had no idea, however, that I wasn't broken. Every time I looked in the mirror, I saw a girl with a fractured smile. I caught his eye and he quickly became infatuated. He made me feel. I hadn't felt anything but betrayal and loss and pain in my lifetime. He made me feel something different. The way he looked at me melted me. I was lost in his gaze. The gaze that captured my soul and roped me, binding the internal legs I had fought so hard to stand on of my own capability. Every person in my life had let me down. I was learning to see in the sunlight. The dark curtain that had been closing in on me was slowly revealing a light I was drawn to. With enlightening perseverance, I had clawed my way back after hitting every jagged edge on the way down to rock bottom, and I let him open the curtain way too fast. It was a whirlwind. He showed me affection, and I lapped it up like a thirsty kitten savoring every last drop of milk. I soaked it in and felt alive for the first time in my young life.

I stood there despondent and numb. I was tired. Soulfully tired. Being abandoned and rejected by the person who brought you into this world and vowed to protect you is all-consuming. I felt worthless and unlovable and alone. I was fragile and delicate, a doll made of glass. I wanted to be seen. I would never amount to enough. He would never choose me. Nobody would choose me.

I lay down, emotionless. The tears no longer flow freely. The pain has become numbness and emptiness. The desire is gone. I'm breathless and beaten; broken. My mind has devoured thoughts of satiety and fulfillment. Hatred, anger and grief have all dissipated. Nothing left. The despair glorifies the forsakenness of my soul. The crown of self-contempt I wear has become jagged and bores into my core. The essence of my being is starved for satisfaction while my heart screams for release. Tossed aside with the unwanted crumbs of greed, I'm despondent. Let me go, my soul whispers. The oneness of my psyche satisfies the greediness of my self-indulgent mindset. There is no other way. Yet, the lack of love and enveloping warmth is prominent and evident. I only got that from you. The voracity for your touch awakens the forbiddenness of it all. I open my eyes and put one foot in front of the other.

CHAPTER TWENTY-THREE

A Monster Was Born - *Age 30*

Somehow, deep in my soul, I knew he wouldn't just leave me be. He doesn't just go away... and I couldn't just walk away. He was a magnet, and for him, I was his obsession. He left me trauma-bonded in some sort of twisted emotional attachment I couldn't sever. Why was my heart so big? Why did I still want to save him? Why did I want to fix him? I was finally catching my breath and seeing the world a little clearer. As I was trying to find my footing and stand on solid ground, the world opened up. The kids were in school and were happy and carefree. They laughed and played and were completely different kids.

Until the texts. And the calls. AFTER we had moved away. AFTER the divorce. He wouldn't leave me alone. It took nearly a year for me to realize he was living close by. The excessive texts dripping verbal assault were almost worse than the physical battery I had endured. The remnants of black eyes, fat lips, and scratches were long healed, but the verbal ambush on my character wore me down. The relentless onslaught of my integrity corroded my veracity until I truly believed I would never be free. He claimed he moved to be closer to the kids because it was difficult not to be with them. In my opinion, he simply couldn't — or refused to — let me go. I only assume this because it's when the stalking began. I couldn't figure out why he was so fixated on me. He had been in other relationships before me and had other children. Why me? What was so captivating about me that he couldn't let me go? I supposed it was because of the way I left. The control was taken from him, and he wasn't finished with me yet.

"Please don't take the kids away from me." He pleaded with me over voicemails and texts. My only request, the same request I'd had for the past handful of years, was that he QUIT DRINKING. *"Whatever you want. Whatever it takes,"* he swore. I believed he could change so much that I paid for some of his rehab. The kids deserved to be more important than a drink. They deserved to be chosen. I never was. I didn't want them to feel that way. I had vowed to give them what I never had, and to make sure they knew they would always come first. After he completed the program, I had hope. It was a virtue I had lost so many times before, but without hope, I had nothing. A court granted him parenting time, and I trusted him. Giving him the benefit of the doubt when he claimed he hadn't made enough money yet to pay his rent, I wanted him to have a place to live so the kids could visit with him. I paid his rent. I was fooled. I believed in him, believed he was better than this. I could fix him. That's what I do. Maybe I just needed a break, or a night out, or to not think about the fact that my ex-husband, the person I trusted and loved the most at one point, had hurt me so badly that I'd fled from him; yet he followed me... another red flag I ignored. Another gut instinct that steered me wrong.

142

Fool me once, shame on you. Fool me twice, shame on me. For several months, he kept the kids every other weekend. He started with one day a month, then Saturday morning to Sunday afternoon, and eventually Friday night to Sunday evening. I could always tell when he had had even one drink. His face changed, his voice changed, and he tried harder to enunciate. When I dropped them off and picked them up, he appeared to be sober. Maybe my nightly prayers were working.

On one of his weekends, I found my daughter's nightly medication on the counter. I must've forgotten to pack it. I called with no answer. Not a problem; perhaps they were out or napping or otherwise not available. I tried again an hour later. No answer. Slightly more concerning, but I was not worried. Another hour, another ignored call. After quite a few more attempts, my calls became more frequent. Texts unread, voicemails unheard, phone unanswered. A quiet weekend at home for me prompted a drive across town. The parenting plan was unambiguously clear: Communication between the parents should be strictly pertinent to the children, non-abusive, and the children should be readily available to the other parent, barring unforeseen circumstances or behavior that warrants limited contact. That clause was more directed towards him, and I often disconnected calls from him when I had the kids, because he couldn't control himself. However, an unforeseen circumstance making him unavailable by phone would still warrant a phone call to me. Typically, the kids know when I'm coming to pick them up and greet me at the window before running down the stairwell. They didn't know I was coming, and the living room they often peeked out to acknowledge me was dark except for the soft flickering glow of the television — unusual for a house with kids at 7PM. The pit in my stomach grew. Knocking softly on the door, I breathed a sigh of relief when I heard my daughter's timid voice sweetly singing to the boys. I knocked a little louder and she gasped. I tried the door, and it was locked. *"Open the door."* I articulated.

"Mommy!!" Noah shouted. Relieved, I rested my head on the door. When it opened, he had his finger to his lips. *"SHHH, Daddy sleeeeeeping."*

He was in the familiar "sleep where he fell" pose: prone position with nothing but a sheet barely covering his naked body and a half-empty bottle of whiskey tucked into his shoe with the neck of the bottle exposed.

"Want to go home?" I whispered to them.

"Yes."

"Mmhmm."

"Yah," they all said in unison.

"Get your stuff," I quietly replied. My daughter was only wearing socks and underwear. *"Where are your clothes?"* She shrugged.

"In the bathroom, I think." I would ask her why later. Noah had only one of his dad's t-shirts on. *"Where are your pants, bud?"* I incredulously asked him. He shrugged. *"I took a baf and my big boy pants are gone,"* his toddler verbiage referred to the underwear he just started wearing all the time. *"Why? It doesn't matter. Do you have a Pull-Up?"* I whispered.

"But I wear big boy pants now."

"I know," I told him. *"Just to get home."* He pointed to the mountain of laundry on the bed. Exasperated, I kissed his little hand that was holding my middle and index fingers. *"It's ok. Let's go home."* Liam was wearing only a full diaper. I decided to change him first, and I really wish I hadn't. My rustling through the mound of dirty clothes to find the diaper bag woke Dan. Pulling Liam's pants on, I tried to usher the kids out the door as fast as I possibly could.

"Why are you here?"

Here we go. Wondering why I couldn't just keep walking and not engage with him infuriates me every time I think of it. Why did I have to acknowledge him?

"I tried calling, but you didn't answer."

"They are fine. Just like always." His words muddled together so I could barely make them out.

"I'm just going to take them home."

"It's my weekend. You can't."

"I can, and I am," I said as I ushered them out the door.

Some name-calling commenced.

"Go to the car." I handed my keys to Chloe and mouthed our family safe word. She knew the drill. Push the button to unlock the car and strap the boys in their car seats. By the time I got this situation handled, they would be safely ready to go.

"It's fine. They will call you tomorrow." I opened his front door and attempted to close it behind me. Barely on the first step, I felt the burning yank at my scalp. A yelp escaped

my lips, but my hand covered my mouth instantly. The kids wouldn't be in the car yet, and I didn't want them to come back up to witness more traumatic events. He pulled me by my hair up the stairs and back into the apartment, slamming the door. Once behind the door, I lashed out.

"LET GO OF ME!" He had a large handful of my hair in his fist and complete control of my head. I was bent over in an L shape with one hand clawing at his to get him to release my hair and the other reaching across my face, digging my nails into his bicep. As he pushed my head further down and pulled my hair further up, the popping sound of the hair being pulled from my scalp and the burning sensation that followed caused me to cry out. I turned my head as slightly as I was able and felt flesh between my teeth. I locked my jaws together as if chomping into a sinewy hunk of meat.

"YEOW!" The bellow came from deep in his belly. *"LET GO!"* I vigorously shook my head.

"You first," I muttered through gritted teeth with solid muscle locked in my bite. The familiar metallic taste of blood filled my mouth. The more he pulled my hair, the harder I bit down. He quickly realized his upward action resulted in skin stretching further against the resistance of my teeth. The very millisecond he loosened his grip, I bolted down the stairs and sped out of the driveway. All three kids were strapped in, none the wiser. The throbbing of my scalp and the burning of my skin was less painful with the lingering salty aftertaste of a penny on my tongue.

To this day, he has a perfect imprint of my bite as a scar on his thigh. If you ask him how he got that, it's a funny rendition that makes him sound like a hero.

Against my better judgment, I let them go with him for another weekend. A court order told me I had to, and I was so straight-and-narrow that it came back to bite me. I equipped Chloe with a basic flip phone with one number programmed into it: Mom.

"Just hold down the number 1 and it will call me."

"Like this?" She inquisitively asked with the cute lisp she inadvertently developed due to her top two teeth missing. Her petite pointer finger punched the number one until her fingertip turned red. My phone vibrated in my pocket. I put it to my ear and answered. *"Hi baby girl."* She beamed, her tongue barely sticking out as she curled her upper lip into a smile that melted my heart. She liked my nickname for her. She knew she would always be my baby — my first born; my only girl. Baby Girl. She never fought it, unlike my youngest baby. *"I'm not a baby anymore,"* he liked to remind me.

They will always be my babies. They knew, even if they wanted to dispute their "baby" status. They were also blessed with my resilience, so they were older than they seemed, with all they had overcome in their young lives that far. Old souls. They were good judges of character. Their opinions held the highest regard. They came before me, before anyone else on the planet, and I wouldn't dare let anyone hurt them. I'm timid, reserved, and standoffish, but I'm also protective and guarded like a mama panda bear: Cute on the outside and will keep to myself unless you mess with my babies; then I'll rip your face off... but still look cute doing it.

"Just like that. You press that button and you call me. I'll be right there." I could sense her relief. We have always been connected in that way. She is my person.

Not even one weekend later, I got a call. I answered on the first ring. *"Hi baby girl."*

"I just wanted to make sure it worked." It broke my heart in two, but I forced a smile. I knew she would notice if I didn't. *"It will always work, baby girl; always."*

She deeply sighed. *"Ok mommy."* It melted me. She only called me mommy when she felt vulnerable. I wanted so badly to let her know I would forever have her back, while also leading her down the correct path. She could enjoy her life being a kid while also knowing that with one press of a button, I would be right there as soon as my phone rang. Forever and always.

There were a few uneventful weekends, and I mistakenly assumed things were on the mend. In exchanging the children, I never went up with them again; instead, I had one of the kids wave to me from the window, letting me know they were in the apartment and okay. My anxiety spiked and my heart heaved each time I pulled away from them. I had false hope that the worst was over. I seemed to be a trigger to him, so I hoped removing myself from the center would ease the flame I seemed to spark. Then, it happened.

Ringing phone. Racing heart. Sweaty palms. Cold sweats. All I wanted to do was protect my babies. Scoop them up in my arms and run far, far away. Safe from corruption and destruction and pain. They didn't need to see his self-destruction. Kids only learn what they're taught. Heaven help me if my kids didn't learn anything but strength, perseverance, and determination, no matter what is staring them down.

Honestly, painfully, I admit I didn't want to answer the phone. For a slight second, I dreamed of running away from it all. But my babies filled my entire soul and nothing was okay in my world until they were at my side. *"Hi baby girl. What's wrong?"*

"Mommy?" Her sugary soprano voice clearly came through the earphone.

"What's wrong?" I was out with some friends and put my hand to my left ear to close it off to outside sounds so I could hear her better. *"It's late, babe, what's going on?"*

"Can you come get us? Please, I want to go home."

"What's going on?"

"Can you please?"

The interrupted silence caught my breath in my throat. *"Baby girl, what's going on?"*

"WHY DID YOU CALL YOUR MOM? HANG UP THE PHONE!" I blatantly heard on the other end.

"Please mommy? Sorry dad," her buttery voice was muffled. She breathed our family safe word as the soft click of her hanging up drummed in my ear. Within seconds of my daughter hanging up with me, the bombardment of text messages commenced. ***Why are you meddling in my parenting time? Why is she calling you? What is she saying? What did she say was going on? We were having a good time. I didn't know she was calling you. Stop brainwashing her. You stole them, this is my weekend. Just stop.***

I texted Chloe a simple response. ***I will be there in the morning. Just try and sleep and I'll be there when you wake*** *up.* I ended it with a simple one word response to our safe word so that she knew I heard her.

Her response was *I don't want to, but ok.*

Just as I promised, I was there first thing the next morning. No longer did I want to force them to spend the entire weekend with him. Little did I know, the decision was about to be made for me.

A random Tuesday the weekend after I wrongly assumed things were on the mend, I came home from work, kids in tow, to a note neatly attached to my door knocker with a single piece of tape. Child Protective Services. *I'm sorry I missed you. Please contact me at your soonest convenience regarding a report made to the Department of Children and Families.* My racing heart immediately made me think aloud, *"Who called on me? What could I have possibly done?"*

Terrified and shaking, I called the number on the letter.

Within an hour, a diminutive woman, professionally dressed with creased white slacks and a blue off-the-shoulder blouse tied at the waist was at my door. Her hair pulled into a tight bun, her serious facial expressions, and her all-business demeanor were intimidating. She proceeded to explain that a report was made, and they are required to investigate all allegations of abuse or neglect. *"Neglect!?"* the word came out a bit higher than my normal octave.

"I'd like to talk to the children separately."

"Um sure. Whatever you need." The knot in my stomach and the lump in my throat were trying to burst their way through my sanctuary of safety. I could hear laughter from their bedroom. The kids were all crammed into one

bedroom right now, and I wondered if I was going to get dinged for that. Was this a test? Did I have enough food? Every other Friday are grocery shopping days. The kids were sharing a room. Noah, at nearly four years old, had just transitioned to a toddler bed, so he was on the bottom bunk of a bunk bed he shared with his sister, and Liam, almost two, had a crib on the other side of the room. At least they had their own beds, but should they have their own space? Should the girl be in the same room with the boys? Did they have enough toys? Didn't the baby fall yesterday, and he has a bump on his head and a scratch on his knee? Did his daycare call them? How could they? They told me he fell! All the irrational and absurd scenarios flooded my mind.

"Mama!" My youngest screeched as he toddled out of the bedroom to show me the Spiderman sticker he just picked out of the prize box the woman offered to each of them.

"May I sit?" She asked, pointing at the chair across from me at my dining room table. I nodded. *"Someone called in an incident regarding your children."*

"Who?" I snapped.

"Unfortunately, since it's an open case, I can't reveal who called it in."

"What did I do?" I started to ask, but she rested her hand on top of mine as the tears fell. *"All I'm trying to do is protect them."*

She interrupted me. *"What I can tell you is that the report wasn't made against you."*

"What?"

I was so confused. *"Since the report is not against you, I can give you a copy of the complaint — just not who made it."*

"OK." I was relieved and angry at the same time. I knew immediately who it was against, but not the circumstance. Did someone see him drinking with the kids in his care? Did someone see him passed out while the kids were with him?

Three days later, the report was ready and in my email.

A call was made to the department. Three young children, one barely walking in just a diaper, outside after midnight playing and running around the swimming pool with no supervision.

Livid, I re-read that sentence. I memorized that sentence because I repeated it over and over and over. Any one of my kids could have fallen in the pool and then what? This was the second time, and I could not trust him anymore. I emailed the caseworker back and asked her what would happen next. She replied quickly and told me that they would be making a visit to him as well to make sure he had sufficient accommodations to have the children overnight. I knew that he didn't. Immediately, I called my attorney — the same one who had represented me in our divorce — and asked about my options, if I had to continue sending my kids to him every other weekend. He advised me to do what I thought was best for my children. This was the second time I was told the exact same thing.

"What happens if I don't send them anymore?" I probed.

"He would have to take you to court and dispute that you aren't following the parenting plan, which we could explain and then ask for supervised visitation."

That sounded good to me. That is exactly what I did, and that was precisely when the barrage of verbal abuse and emotional abuse commenced, abuse which still hasn't ceased.

CHAPTER TWENTY-FOUR

The Stalking - *Age 30*

Weeks went by with no contact. He hadn't had overnights with the children since that weekend. The chime on my phone caught my attention. *"How busy is the grocery store?"* It had come the second I walked through the automatic doors. A chill crept up my spine. Looking over my shoulder and quickly scanning the perimeter of the parking lot, I considered leaving. I needed groceries, though, and as I dissected the text message, I presumed he was not inside the store. I felt safer in public, so I surreptitiously shopped. Attempting to reach the Cheerios just out of my grasp, I flinched when a tall stranger reached above my head to grab the box.

"WHOA." He gingerly set the cereal down to a reachable level and backed away with his hands up.

"I'm sorry, so sorry," my voice cracked.

"You ok?" He asked concernedly. Simultaneously, I nodded and shook my head, and that made me look like a

bobble-head. He snickered and said, *"Be careful."* I shuddered. I thanked him and hurried off without looking back.

Cereal, milk, juice, bread, frozen pizza. Good enough. With so many items forgotten, I suddenly just wanted out of the store and to be at home with the kids. If he was somewhere close by, I didn't want him to follow me to the kids' schools or to my house. Taking the long route, I intently watched cars around me to ensure I wasn't being followed. I'm honestly not sure what felt worse: being imprisoned in my own home with an anticipated fight each night or being trapped in my outside world, living every day in perpetual fear of the unknown. Where was he? What was he doing? Was he watching me? Did he know where I lived? Where I worked? Who my friends were? Did he know what the kids were doing? Did he know I was terrified, yet vehemently attempting to denote confidence and control my own emotions each time he spewed profanity and taunted me with his threats? I pretended to be unaffected, but he didn't know I still slept with my shoes on, and that I needed a night light in order to sleep. Years later, I still needed complete silence in order to fall asleep so that I could hear every sound and prepare for what my mind believed was inevitable. I was living in a constant state of fight-or-flight which left me perpetually exhausted. I blocked his phone number. For several days, I felt relief. He called and texted from a different phone number. I blocked seven different numbers until finally I changed mine. He somehow obtained it. My next objective was to find the mole.

CHAPTER TWENTY-FIVE

My Realization - *Age 30*

The day came when he couldn't even get through a day without needing a sip. A sip turned into a swig, then a guzzle, then the whole bottle. He lacked self-control. Restraint was a foreign concept. He often left before any of the rest of us were up in the morning. I never slept very soundly. I heard the click of the cap before I heard the coffee maker brewing. I wasn't stupid; I just chose to ignore it. The more oblivious I pretended to be, the more peacefully I lived. Painting on an ignorant façade, I put my blinders on and followed my schedule. A problem is only a problem when you address it; at least, that was my perspective. He was compassionate and affectionate and romantic. He was drinking away from me and leaving me alone. For as long as I could remember, the routine was to get the kids off to school, but before I planned anything for my day, I'd wait for him to call. Every weekday morning at 8:30 AM, he'd call just as he got his work for the day. He would let me know where he was working, how long he thought it would take, and what time he would be home. I don't think he had any idea how valuable that information was. The most stressful part of my day was calculating my timeline. He was a skilled electrician and would sometimes obtain impressive work orders he seemed thrilled to tackle. He was very good at his job.

The calls eventually stopped. Sometimes he got off early and sometimes there was just no work, but it changed from day to day and I wasn't privy to that information anymore.

I assumed he quit that job to follow us. Once he arrived, he obtained a job from a friend of his who wanted to help him after he had painted the picture that I left him destitute and heartbroken for absolutely no reason.

At the shop where his friend hired him, he had very little interaction with guests. I'm not sure if this was an advantage or disadvantage for him. He told me he took this job because it was the only job he could get — a job that was beneath him — because I ruined his career. He had expertise and experience in the electrical field, but apparently a domestic violence charge on his record was grounds for immediate termination. He said it made him unhireable.

Once I left, I did not follow up on his job status. The only reason I knew the status of the charges was that the District Attorney called me. They were dropping the charges because I was no longer in the county, and he had taken a plea. I had never felt more dismissed — even when my mother discarded me — than when I saw the police fail to deem me worthy of protection.

One quiet Friday night at home, the kids and I were watching a Toy Story marathon. I was lying on the couch using

Chloe's lap as a pillow for my legs, my mama's boy was curled up behind my head with his little hand in mine, and Liam was lying next to me with his blanket up to his little chin and covering my hip. Passing the popcorn bowl around, Chloe turned her head towards the window.

"Someone's here!"

"Someone's here?" I craned my neck to look out the window as headlights glared into my living room. *Who is that? I said in my head.* Within seconds, a loud knock at my door startled all of us. *"SHH. It's ok."* Wriggling my way out of the maze the kids and I had created on the couch, I looked through the peephole. Groaning loudly, I opened the door just enough to see Dan standing outside the door. He could barely stand. *"What. Do. You. Want?"* I said through gritted teeth, visibly irritated. He tried to speak but couldn't put a sentence together.

"How do you know where I live?"

"Lemme see my kids." I think is what he said. Placing his hand on my door to try and push it open, he was stopped by the chain lock. Without wanting to let him know I was scared, I forcibly asked him to leave. I slammed my door, locked the deadbolt, and turned all the lights off. I watched him drive away, straight through the neighbor's yard. I don't know why I didn't call the police and turn him in for drunk driving. I was just relieved he left. As I looked at my kids, wide-eyed and looking up at me, I still had a soft spot I couldn't explain for that man. We moved the movie party to my room, and the tears fell silently as they each fell asleep wrapped snugly in my arms. There was no place I would rather be, and there was no battle I wouldn't fight to make sure they knew it.

CHAPTER TWENTY-SIX

Recovery - *Age 31*

I lived in fear, not just that he wouldn't let me go, or of something happening, but for the world, my children, and my safety net. Fear consumed me. Not the deathly afraid, shaking, uncontrollable fear, but the silent kind. The kind of fear that envelopes your soul. The kind that takes over every good intention, every good emotion, every good thought that comes to your mind. The fear that annihilated my being, the kind that reminds you no matter how 'together' you have it, or seem to have it, you ultimately have no control over anything. I became dejected, deprived, and robbed of my own self-worth. I was a shell of a person and succumbed to depression.

Depression is no joke. Depression can lie dormant for years and then hit hard, fast, and seemingly out of nowhere. It's overwhelming, overpowering, and unkind. It consumes you. It tells you everything you don't like about yourself. It tells you there is no way out. It makes you believe that no matter what you do, it isn't enough. I fell into a deep, dark depression, a spiraling hole of despair. Nothing mattered. I lost interest in everything I loved doing. I was living each day simply going through the motions. I wasn't me. I looked like me, but I didn't feel like me. I looked forward to absolutely nothing. I was unsure each morning when I woke up whether I was going to be content, downright angry, or completely despondent. I had no control over my emotions and no idea why. How could one person have this much power over how I felt about myself? Feelings of helplessness and powerlessness overtook me. I felt myself changing, and not in the way I wanted to. I acquiesced to this new normal, but in reality, I had become cold. Emotionless. I felt nothing at all. I was a different kind of shell. I couldn't cry. I couldn't laugh. I was stoic. I was no longer in fear, but instead I was hollow. Things still didn't seem to matter, but I didn't care. With no energy or zest for life, my drive was stalled. Easily affected by other people and how they made me feel, I faltered. I lost all control of my emotions, my thought processes, my being. I felt the fight in me dwindling, but I was not going to let this win.

Watching a movie with my kids one night, their laughter, playful chatter, and random dancing sparked something in me. I had removed danger from their lives once before, and they were happy! I wanted better than this; I needed to be better for them. I would not let this define me. I had to prove to my children that we won. We won the war. I desired more out of life, to enjoy my newfound freedom and everything that entailed. I wanted to enjoy my children while they were still little, and to feel happy baking, reading, writing, and tasting wine again. I wanted to relish in making my own money and not answering to anybody. I could finally do what I wanted with my own life, not just survive or "get through it," but thrive. I simply wanted to FEEL again.

Anything. They deserved it, and why didn't I? I worked so hard to get to this point single-handedly, so why did he still get to destroy it? I didn't deserve to feel unworthy. I refused to let this re-mold my life and my being and turn me into someone I wasn't. I was fixed on finding my own worth and discovering who I was before this, and who I wanted to be from this point on. I needed to relearn how to love myself. Everybody who had hurt me did not get to choose my direction. I had overcome so much already; how was this any different? It hurt immensely more, but I knew in the core of my being that I could conquer this. Love doesn't conquer all. Self-worth does.

Making the decision to get better — which is harder than it sounds — I sought help. You can't just tell your mind to shut off or to change its way of thinking. You don't wake up one day and suddenly feel better, but it's a start, to wake up one day and WANT to be better. Slowly falling into this hole took months, if not years; I knew it would take many months to get out. The first step is realizing something isn't right, and then comes taking the next step to change it. I'm still a work in progress but have come so far already. I had to continually tell myself that I am enough. I've always been enough, and I will always be enough. At the end of my journey, I couldn't wait to see myself as I was meant to be. The sun got a little brighter. My children's hugs were a little warmer. My life was a little sweeter. My heart was a little fuller. It's important for me to realize that. Where I came from, where I went, and where I'm going. I had to remind myself that this was a snapshot of my life. A snapshot that would take me the longest to recover from, and that would leave the biggest imprint. But I knew it was time to retake the picture.

CHAPTER TWENTY-SEVEN

Healing - Age 33

I am not ashamed to say that I needed therapy. I proudly maintain that I have a therapist. I couldn't do this on my own. We aren't designed to. It takes a village to raise a child, but it also takes a community to nurture you so you can blossom. I am so thankful for my tribe, my circle of friends who have waited for me to heal, waited for me to see my own value, and walked with me through some of the worst years of my life. Support from people who see you is underrated. If you don't sit with me in the "suck," don't expect me to let you celebrate with me in the "good." My therapist told me it would take twice as long as the abuse lasted to recover from it. The relationship lasted a total of five years. I am ten years out of it now and barely beginning to function normally, where every demeaning description for me he spews, every word he speaks, and every insult he drools isn't soul-draining and doesn't batter my entire being. It's a cognitive change like I've never experienced before. What others think of me has often defined me, for the people that were supposed to love me the most destroyed me the greatest.

Verbal and emotional abuse leaves scars that can't be covered with makeup or a turtleneck sweater. Any trigger of mine — even those I wasn't aware of — resulted in an unforgettable basketball of words dribbling in my brain. In the middle of a bad day, or a moment of self-doubt, every attack on my character and well-being reverberated piercingly in my head until I started to believe it. Every chance he got, he would reiterate how unlovable I was or undesirable I would be as a single mother. He made it a priority to point out every single one of my flaws to remind me I was mediocre at best.

I suffered silently through this from afar for years. His constant blubbering of how worthless I am, or how unwanted I would be made me believe I would never truly be free. He was in my head. The text messages used language so vulgar even the judge was appalled, and I was granted a restraining order.

Eventually, the only option was to get as far away from him as possible. Moving across the country is THE best thing I could have done. The kids needed a better life and a mother who was strong and could overcome any obstacle. I was determined to show them, even at their young ages, that I was a fighter, and I would not go down without a fight. I needed a chance at healing. They needed a mother who could and would do anything for them. He still takes his shots every chance he gets, but he must work harder to push that button. I'm trying hard to find forgiveness and understanding in a way that won't depreciate what I went through, but feeling empathy for him won't allow acceptance of his behavior. My true healing will come when I can look him in the eye, tell him

I forgive him, and mean it. I'm not there yet, but I'm not afraid of him anymore. I took my control and my power back. He's not a bad guy. I don't want to portray him as a monster — only an abuser who made poor decisions that affected my ability to fully trust and confidently rely on others. Though I doubt the bruises left behind on my heart and soul will ever truly be healed, I've forgiven him for his actions to the extent I need to in order to move forward.

FINAL THOUGHTS

It does take time, but it does get better. Sometimes it feels like it never will. Patience, energy, strength, and comfort will feel far-fetched. Exhaustion, defeat, overwhelming powerlessness, and desperation will be at the forefront. But determination, perseverance, tenacity, and your purpose will overcome. You will see that you are worthy, loved, and stronger than you ever knew. You are enough. You are more than enough. Find it within you, find your reason, and run with it.

I didn't believe that I would ever be okay. Every time I heard his voice in my head telling me I would not be able to survive on my own, raise kids on my own, or ever be worthy of anything, the more I wanted to prove I would, not to him, but to me. I COULD do this. I realized that if I could spend the majority of my life suffering, just trying to get through the next debilitating thing and not be hardened to the world, and not become cruel and full of hate and anger and resentment, then I was a force to be reckoned with. I could do anything. I had to start believing that. It was that moment when I recognized I had a story to tell, and somebody needed to hear it.

There is life after a lifetime of pain, despair, and heartache. It's up to you to determine what you do with it.

I can also tell you that there is love after, too. True love. The kind that makes you forget there was ever evil in your world. I found it. I finally have a good guy. My kids don't scare him. My baggage doesn't scare him. My triggers don't scare him. My messy, disorganized, chaotic, and cluttered past doesn't scare him. Except for a chronic illness that keeps him from conquering the world with me, he is the epitome of perfection. There is a proper way to be loved. There is a man out there who will love you. There is someone out there who will treat you the way you should be treated. Every woman deserves to be put first. You matter. And the man who sees you as his other half will prove that to you. I met my true knight in shining armor through mutual friends. And I couldn't be more thankful for them. I was sitting with my friend on a girls' night out and she jokingly asked me, "Are you going to marry him?"

"Maybe," I said. When you know, you know. And I knew. When you are loved correctly, the entire world changes.

It's difficult to love someone through demanding circumstances that require energy and strength which far exceed your capacity, but when you are loved correctly, you want to. Let me tell you about that.

www.ingramcontent.com/pod-product-compliance
Lightning Source LLC
Chambersburg PA
CBHW060522130626

46553CB00002B/613